What People Are Say

In Search of Hope

This little book offers really helpful resources to anyone searching for hope in these turbulent times. Drawing on her own experience, Joanna Godfrey Wood expertly weaves together stories, personal reflections, and simple practices that help us to keep focused on a light that shines in the darkness. This is needed now more than ever.

Stuart Masters, Programme Coordinator (History and Theology), Woodbrooke, Birmingham, UK

In Search of Hope is a vibrant, practical book, which draws on the deep roots of the Quaker tradition to provide immediate and useful spiritual help. Through story, example, personal reflection and history the reader is guided on an exploration of the living hope which was experienced by Margaret Fell and which we can experience today.

Rhiannon Grant, Deputy Programme Leader, Centre for Research in Quaker Studies, Woodbrooke, Birmingham, UK, and Honorary Senior Lecturer, University of Birmingham, UK

Joanna Godfrey Wood offers a highly readable exploration of what it means to live an actively hopeful life. By cultivating "witnessing," a special kind of attentiveness to the apparent ordinariness of everyday life, hope can be found as an energizing power in the present. This is a practical book grounded in both the wisdom of early Quaker Margaret Fell and stories of contemporary life. Readers searching for spiritual sustenance and revival in a difficult world will find much to enjoy and draw on here.

Mark Russ, author of *Quaker Shaped Christianity*, Quaker Quicks

In Search of Hope is a packet of seeds. As you read you are gently encouraged to plant these seeds in your own soul and you never know what will germinate and blossom. When you re-read you may find that the stories stay the same but the exercises change each time, because your responses grow into something new and often unexpected. Don't try to skim-read this book and don't read it in one gulp. It's far too rich and will give you spiritual indigestion. It will hopefully become a favorite gift which gives the reader a sense of true communication with other seeking souls.

Frances Sutherland, Resident Quaker, Muswell Hill Meeting, North-West London Area Meeting, UK

"Perhaps hope is a continuing 'forward propulsion', found in the unexpected."
I took this part-sentence as a very helpful focus as I read Joanna Godfrey Wood's book *In Search of Hope*. As an arts psychotherapist I believe that depression or an inner world of negative chatter can kill "hope." Joanna, in a simple and engaging way, involves the reader in a series of vignettes and exercises to connect to meaningful and beautiful moments of being in the "flow" of hope. The book says that if we can only stop and listen mindfully beyond the busy-ness of our lives and our minds, within the stillness is the bigger picture of hope and positivity – and she gives us many tools to aid that experience.

Isa L. Levy, Quaker artist and arts psychotherapist

The unique way the author addresses the complex concept of hope means that the book begins with questions and ends with challenges. Looking at hope using personal stories means readers are allowed their own understandings and perspectives. In this way we can better understand Margaret Fell's and the author's own ideas about hope. The use of creativity, sometimes discouraged within Quakerism, is positively promoted here.

So often a book will talk "at" us with its philosophy. This book suggests creative ways to find our hope, and ourselves. It asks us questions, encourages us to try things, observe things, to stop, to look, to listen. To live adventurously.

Clair Chapwell, writer and arts facilitator, member of Muswell Hill Meeting, North-West London Area Meeting, UK

In Search of Hope

A Personal Quaker Journey

Other books by Joanna Godfrey Wood

Travelling in the Light: How Margaret Fell's Writings Can Speak to Quakers Today
ISBN 978-0-9933627-6-7

In STEP with Quaker Testimony: Simplicity, Truth, Equality and Peace — Inspired by Margaret Fell's Writings
ISBN 978-1-78904-577-2

Margaret Fell was an inspiring and practical leader in the early Quaker movement in seventeenth-century England. Remembered as the wife of George Fox, her writings have been largely forgotten. This book brings them to life again, with excerpts and reflections structured around the four testimonies that have continued to shape Quaker witness to this day: Simplicity, Truth, Equality and Peace. To do this, Joanna Godfrey Wood follows each passage with a modern adaptation of Fell's words and then explores her own personal responses from a twenty-first-century perspective. We are left with a sense of a strong and beautiful bridge linking past and present.

Joanna Godfrey Wood's appropriate "bringing to new light" of the essence of Margaret Fell's central texts is a major Quaker re-discovery.
Alec Davison, a founder of the Leaveners, Quaker Quest, and The Kindlers
This is a fascinating book, a unique blend of reminiscence, commentary and Quaker wisdom.
Geoffrey Durham, author of *What Do Quakers Believe?*

In Search of Stillness: Using a Simple Meditation to Find Inner Peace
ISBN 978-1-78904-707-3

How can we find inner stillness in our lives today? What is it for and how can we use it? Inspired by the fiery writings of early Quakers, such as George Fox and Margaret Fell, this book calls on their advice to go within and wait, adapting it to create a modern, relatable method for finding stillness and peace. This meditation is for us to use however we most need it, whether to explore and heal the self and others or to help us be more effective in the wider world.

This book is filled with good ideas about how we can use stillness as part of a daily practice of contemplation, wellbeing, and action in the world. Drawing on a selection of inspiring early Quaker writings, Joanna translates the insights of those prophets into modern usage so we can all discover the potential of silence and stillness in our everyday lives.

Ben Pink Dandelion, Programmes Leader, Centre for Research in Quaker Studies, Woodbrooke, Birmingham, UK, and Professor of Quaker Studies, University of Birmingham, UK

In Search of Stillness is a creative and practical book of Liberal Quaker spirituality. In imaginatively adapting a simple meditation in a wide variety of ways, Joanna makes a central insight into the Liberal Quaker tradition accessible to modern-day seekers.

Mark Russ, Quaker educator, theologian and blogger, author of *Quaker Shaped Christianity*

In Search of Hope

A Personal Quaker Journey

Joanna Godfrey Wood

CHRISTIAN ALTERNATIVE
BOOKS

Winchester, UK
Washington, USA

JOHN HUNT PUBLISHING

First published by Christian Alternative Books, 2024
Christian Alternative Books is an imprint of John Hunt Publishing Ltd.,
No. 3 East St., Alresford, Hampshire SO24 9EE, UK
office@jhpbooks.com
www.johnhuntpublishing.com
www.christian-alternative.com

For distributor details and how to order please visit the 'Ordering' section on our website.

Text copyright: Joanna Godfrey Wood 2023

ISBN: 978 1 80341 514 7
978 1 80341 525 3 (ebook)
Library of Congress Control Number: 2023933871

A CIP catalogue record for this book is available from the British Library.

Design: Stuart Davies

UK: Printed and bound by CPI Group (UK) Ltd, Croydon, CR0 4YY
US: Printed and bound by Thomson-Shore, 7300 West Joy Road, Dexter, MI 48130

We operate a distinctive and ethical publishing philosophy in all areas of our business, from our global network of authors to production and worldwide distribution.

Contents

For Kathleen Gage

*Therefore all turn to the voice that calls you, this is the way, walk
in it: And that which turns and draws your minds towards God,
the Light, which cometh from the Father of Light turn to,
and there will ye witness a living Hope.*
Margaret Fell

Foreword

About Margaret Fell and hope

This book is inspired by the writings of early Quaker Margaret Fell, in particular her words about hope and her phrase "there will ye witness a living Hope" (p. xi).

Margaret Fell (1614–1702), one of the first Quakers and certainly the best-known female Friend from the era of early Quakerism, has long been affectionately called the "mother of Quakerism," though this may be to suggest a weaker supporting role, which she might, today, fail to recognize. Her role was surely an equal, shared leadership with George Fox and the other first Friends. She opened up her home to visiting itinerant seekers and preachers, common during the English Civil War, presumably finding herself in a place of personal spiritual questing. Her household became a vital hub for the establishment of the early Quaker movement and she had the means, as a member of the gentry, to be generous to those who needed her hospitality. By the end of her life she had written a vast collection of vital campaigning and theological work, which is gathered together in one volume known as, *A brief collection of remarkable passages and occurrences relating to the birth, education, life, conversion, travels, services, and deep sufferings of that ancient, eminent, and faithful servant of the Lord, Margaret Fell*, J. Sowle, 1710.

Fell was born in 1614, was married firstly to Judge Thomas Fell (1632) and secondly, following Judge Fell's death, to George Fox (born 1624). Fox was one of the most well-known founders of Quakerism in the mid-seventeenth century. Between 1633 and 1653 Fell and Judge Fell had eight children and Margaret ran a large estate at Swarthmoor at a time of great religious and social crisis, both physical and spiritual, in England. Fell endured long imprisonments and suffered greatly for her faith and actions, which included campaigning, traveling in ministry, and holding meetings at her home. She died in 1702, aged 88.

"Witness a living hope" (p. xi) is a stand-out phrase in Fell's writings, representing a practical way in which we, all of us, can work on ourselves, in our own lives, so that we are able to draw sustenance from the everyday and be able to persevere in this act by standing in the Light, or perhaps even just by turning toward it. Fell's witness was to be active, and to act on her leadings, to be practical – whether in her home life or in her public life. She lived by seeing what needed to be done, then doing it, and by finding hope in her actions. In our own ways, we can in turn witness her life and find our own hope in our own actions.

Acknowledgments

Grateful thanks to Isa Louise Levy, Frances Sutherland, and Carol Scott, members of The Writing Hub (2020–), for their wise feedback and encouragement. Also, to Ann Berne, and to Sally Wright for creating the cover collage.

Thanks go to Ruth Tod and Tracey Martin for their insightful comments. Thanks also to Mark Cohen, Rhiannon Grant, Stuart Masters, Mark Russ, Neliana Fuenmayor and Clair Chapwell. Thanks, also, to the other Quaker Quicks authors for their companionship and support. Last, but by no means least, heartfelt thanks to the team at Christian Alternative Books for their guidance and patience.

Introduction

Searching for hope

What does "hope" mean? What does it mean to *have* hope? How can we nurture that often transient feeling, which can be there one moment but gone the next? How can we notice it and find it in our everyday lives? How can we see that we *do* have hope and how can we use it to benefit life in big ways and small? We want hope, we have to believe that there is hope, we need it, we must have it in order to continue, but how can we find it and then hold on to it, even if only for a split-second of uplift? Perhaps hope is a continuing forward propulsion, found in the unexpected, the quirky and the surprising, rather than in rainbows, hearts, and flowers. And perhaps hope can be arrived at in the practice of waiting, listening, discerning, and acting in the silence and the stillness.

Throughout life we are constantly remembering experiences, both meaningful and of little seeming significance, and reliving them. How do we learn from those experiences? How does remembering enable hope to flourish within? How can we carry on hoping? A Quaker answer might be found in Fell's writings: we can wait faithfully in the Light, learning all our lives and recalling our experience, so that we live in a continuing renewal of the cycle of a life full of hope. This is to live, if we can, an experimenting, exploring sort of life, discounting nothing, even if the experience seems on the face of it lacking meaning or worth. When we follow the Quaker practice of sitting in silence, in stillness, with others, waiting on God, we are giving hope the space to flourish in our lives. We have the opportunity to take a step back from the quotidian and let discernment of the self sweep us up in hope, at least for an hour. Hope is already alive in us, and it can be brought out of its slumber when we sit, discern, test, and act – and then we can do it all again, over and over. If we have the faith, grounded in Light, to keep doing this, hope surely stays alive in us.

The usual practice in unprogrammed Quaker meetings is to sit in silence as a group, to wait in the Light (the Divine, Presence, Spirit, God, etc.), without direction or particular focus and see where we might be led. People may spontaneously get to their feet to speak, to minister, sharing what they are led in their hearts to express in the moment. There is no agenda, or order of service, only a will to wait together in the stillness, in worship, to see what is revealed in the Light. This is also a chance to stand back from daily life and an opportunity to be guided by Spirit into reflection, insight, which perhaps leads to revelation. From this may come action, charged with hope, in the world.

Wisdom from the past

Old writings, from centuries ago, from the perspective of our own life and times in the twenty-first century, can be relevant, enriching and facilitating growth for us now, today. It can be easy to dismiss outdated language and expression as being too obscure and difficult, or layered with meaning that seems too complex to unravel. Then there is the feeling that one might have misunderstood or misinterpreted what the writer seems to be saying. And it is easy to feel that the way people thought "then" might have been somehow different to the way they think "now," that we perhaps do things differently in response to modern-day circumstances. But is this really true? This might be to miss the essence of what the writer is trying to say and to fail to benefit from all the things we have in common as human beings.

Words are sent down the centuries to us from other lives, from other times, but they are written for us just as much as for the readers of that time.

Words from Margaret Fell

A paragraph written by Margaret Fell (p. xi) leapt out. In its original context, it is almost buried within a long, complex, sometimes admonishing-seeming text and these few lines cherry-pick the uplifting bits, possibly ignoring the rest. What came before and after seems not to matter so much. At face value, these words are about following instinct and listening to an inner voice, which advises, sometimes in the softest whisper, hardly noticed, and sometimes in the loudest shout, so that one has to pay attention. We have to do what the words say; there is no alternative. Turning to the "light" cast by paying heed to this voice can lead us onward to experiencing real, active hope, which is life itself, and our effective action is a part of it.

A personal response

This book is a response to, and meditation on, the brief phrase "witnessing a living hope." For a long time there was the desire to write about these three words and all the ideas springing from them, but what, how, or in what form was perplexing. There was a need to take time, to meditate on these ideas, slowly and gradually. What might happen? What might emerge? What could be learnt? There was a desire to go into the depths and surface again, richer in life and possibly with something to pass on too. For a long time there seemed to be nothing. No hope, in fact. Not one single word arrived that could be written down and shaped into something. Then what had felt meaningful and heartfelt in the moment seemed nonsense on re-reading. There was no way back into whatever lay behind those words and what had prompted them. Eventually, slowly, there came the realization that the insecurity of *not* knowing, *not* understanding, *not* finding answers had to be lived through, and instead there had to be a listening for leadings and promptings. So used are we to living in the head, to thinking and analyzing, reading and understanding, applying the brain, that this position can be hard to take. Not knowing and moving from a head to a heart position was the way to go. This was a big step.

The questing process

The process of searching without necessarily finding could be an enjoyable, even fulfilling, process. It was questing, though through the practical use of words. It was a focus and a form of meditation. Again and again there was the need to sit down and meditate, think, read, and write. This part of the process had to be extended, with the possibility of never discovering anything at all. Landing in the right mental place to write from, where slivers of awareness lay half-concealed, were times that didn't come along very often. There were many episodes of feeling that there was nothing to say, or if there was something, it seemed impossible to articulate. In the end, perseverance was part of the experience as well as releasing the self from the wagging finger of the inner judge. There had to be self-given freedom to see that there was no right or wrong way of interpreting the three words "witnessing," "living," and "hope," or of expressing what there was to say. It just "was" and is a personal way of doing it.

In looking at the three words "witnessing," "living," and "hope," as well as the phrase as a whole, there seemed to be meaning in the exploration of these things and in discovery. There was encouragement and learning in everyday life that had not been appreciated before. Witnessing turned out to be all about looking for, noticing, being aware of, being attentive to, and finding constructive ways to find hope. The little things of life, past and present, offered great solace. The process of looking within opened up a path of possibility for hope and a creative way, journey, or pathway that seemed to lead somewhere positive and hope-ful. An aim of this book is to offer a positive path to others too, seeking and finding what Margaret Fell refers to as Light, which is her "guide for living."

Perhaps hope lies at an ill-defined point on the intersection of the crossroads where witnessing and living meet with our will and our ability to turn toward the Light.

How this book might work

This book is a practical guide toward living in creative action, prompted by the inner guide, which can, in turn, prompt how we can "witness living hope." It is about integrating Quaker practice, belief, and faith into everyday life. There are personal anecdotes framed as short stories to act as inspiration, as well as practical exercises to try out. The aim is to witness hope and live it out, for the good of the self and for others, to bring more positivity into the world; it is to help make faith a living action that we can embody in our lives today. It is also hoped that this activity steers us further toward our truth, grounded in modern Quakerism. The book is also a meditation on Fell's quote (p. xi), with inspiration for how to "witness a living hope," starting from where we are now and feeling positive about the future. There are practical ideas; some that take place within, and some outwardly in the world; some are outlandish, some perhaps more ordinary, using a mixture of creative projects and practical ideas. The questions do not have to be looked at in order and the stories are episodes from just one life. Yours will be different, of course. These questions have offered hope, and perhaps will for others too, or act as a reminder of different personal life episodes. The exercises, which are only loosely attached to the stories and can be tried randomly, have been found to offer hope too. They are practical ways to work and they do not have to be done in sequence. They are just examples that work for one person – but perhaps they will provide inspiration and ideas for others too, by looking at the smaller practices and habits of life. They are designed to create a space for slowing down and perhaps looking at life in a different and more positive way. That is the hope, and perhaps one of the places where it might be found. They are offered in the spirit of visualizing visions for the future. Pick and choose what appeals to you most and go from there. Listen to your moods and inclinations. Which direction do *you* want to move in? Listen to your heart rather than your head and work from instinct. Think of the themes as a way of changing how you look at the world and use them to guide you in thinking about your own life.

Take this book slowly, perhaps choosing the material that speaks to you personally. This is not a start-to-finish project, so there is no need to read from beginning to end – there is an overlapping and merging of ideas, which perhaps could add up to something more. Take the themes one day at a time, go slowly – see if hope can emerge from shadows.

The book is written partly from a place of wanting to find hope after a difficult time: there has to be hope; there *must* be hope. There is nothing else *but* hope.

The Quaker context

The Society of Friends, Quakers, or at least the "liberal," unprogrammed, branch of it, largely practiced in the UK, USA, and Australia, are known for their "quiet" way of worship, based on silence and stillness, and also their action in the world in their drive for justice and societal change, practical activism, and their caring work with and for others. Modern Quakers do not generally stand in public places loudly proclaiming the word of God and the truth in the fiery manner of the very earliest Friends in the seventeenth century. Though perhaps they should.

Finding hope in the group process

This book aims to help us find hope in ourselves, where we are now, taking the view that hope is a strongly felt personal resource, and holding on to it, finding it for others and ultimately sharing it. It is about constant renewal and the expression of faith. It is about falling in love with life, again, and again, and again. When Quakers say "I hope so" in the process of discernment they are trying to arrive at a decision for the good of all – individuals and community. They say it in the hope, not the assumption, that the will of God is there, in that moment, and with all those present (the "meeting"), and that it prevails in the decision about an issue being explored. This is because we can only act in good faith that something is the right decision. We may not exactly know what is right and what is not right and certainly no one individual can possibly have that certainty and tell others what to do. We can only wait for group clarity and that this, for us, for now, is so. We have to trust the process. In decision-making, in particular, it is better *not* to know, in one's own mind, *not* to be certain, but rather to let the ego go and surrender to the will of God for the good of the group. This has the effect of making us look outward, beyond our small selves. If the decision then turns out to be wrong or mistaken it can be revisited and adjusted using the same methods. This is an expression of hope.

Finding hope in the self

The experience of hope may come in a flash of uplifting feelings, fleeting but raising spirits out of a difficult place, so that the day takes on a different hue and life can go on in a better, more positive, vein. Everything seems easier and lighter than before. It is like seeing the other side of something, revealed for the first time. It all makes sense in a moment of clarity. But we have to hold on to the awareness that we must go in a downward direction in order to come up again. We have to go into the dark before emerging into light. So we cannot have light without dark. They coexist; part of the same whole.

The quote "witnessing a living hope" (p. xi) speaks directly, exhorting us to listen to the inward guide for help, giving insights and nudges as to how we might do this, relying on what we can find within, looking at what is revealed by the Light and finding the hope that is already there, though perhaps lying dormant. The work starts from where we are now, where we find ourselves, in our local meetings, in our relationships with others, in our everyday lives. Things cannot always run smoothly – but we live in hope that we can solve and improve, and gradually find a way. Sometimes we get reverse after reverse and feel hope-less. Lack of hope can take the life out of life, making us feel that things can never change. We feel stuck and unsure how we can persevere or press forward.

Needing to find hope

Trains pass the window all the time. Sometimes quiet passenger trains, other times noisy, cumbersome goods trains. Some carry cars and vans, others containers. Some are so heavy that they shake the house. There are logos, legends, and slogans on the container sides. Some carry the single word "Hope." The letters are red and blue, several feet tall. If the word "Hope" is missed the first time, another one, on another container, comes along. "Hope, hope, hope." It speaks, and seems to say, "Carry on hoping."

This book was written from a place of wanting to find hope, of seeking it, in times of difficulty, when resilience was much needed but seemed distant, even unreachable. Hope was glimpsed, far away, a circle of brightness in the sometimes counter-intuitive juxtapositions of everyday life. The activity of writing was an act of hope in itself. It is hoped that by looking at an oddball collection of life events and memories, random and mundane, examples of hope can be seen with new eyes and offer inspiration and encouragement.

The phrase that comes before

Before focusing on the phrase "witnessing a living hope," looking at the phrase directly before it is useful: "Therefore all turn to the voice that calls you, this is the way, walk in it" (p. xi).

This seems to have the power to wake us up from a patch of boredom, a depression, negativity, a place of not knowing, from impatience and frustration. These are all things that can pull us down and leave us floundering, uncertain about which way to turn. The phrase seems to contain energy, alerting us to something that we *can* do – now. Rather than looking toward the negative, perhaps, it is encouraging us to turn instead to something outward, upward, positive, which can give immediate inspiration, assistance – and hope. There is a path to move toward, pointing the way, and encouraging us to follow. The voice is whatever personal experience and interpretation we might find inwardly and outwardly – the self, the inner voice, the outer voice. Something might be prompting us toward action – somehow. There may be no need to put a label on it, but to just hold an awareness of an inward direction, a prompt. Not only is there an encouragement to find a way but also to "walk" in it – not just "on" its surface but "in" it; to "inhabit" it. Hope is already there, but it just has to be recognized and experienced within. It is about finding hope for the self and for others: finding hope and then holding on to it and sharing it with others. It is about constant renewal.

Chapter 1

Witnessing

[T]here will ye witness a living Hope.
Margaret Fell

"Witnessing" includes noticing and observing but it also has woven into it a personal responsibility, to what is happening around us, and within us too. It is to become part of the action rather than just being there at the time and seeing. It is being attentive, absorbing what is there, remembering and also manifesting or bringing to life the broad range of our experience. Witnessing can be deeply felt. Perhaps it is an experience of living right inside something, and of being awake and aware to it. It is how we respond to all of life, to the big things and to the little things. Perhaps witnessing is also to do with deep listening, with the whole of our selves. It is to see what is already truly present and to take it on in full, to bring it to one's self. Within, there is the possibility of searching for, finding, witnessing hope. Perhaps we can abandon thoughts and images that do not serve us in finding our witness and employ others that do, with an openness of heart and in a spirit of creativity.

"Witnessing" hope, as Margaret Fell states, is not about thinking about hope in the usual sense of engaging the brain, of wanting things or feeling hopeful or uttering prayers of petition. It instead seems to broaden out the idea of hope. Rather than hoping for the self it seems to be hoping for the good of all of life. Hope is already there, everywhere in existence. For example, the witness of hope in springtime each year is there in buds forming, with the promise of the certainty of green leaves fluttering later on.

At Easter we may witness inwardly, on some level, the resurrection of Christ; a re-birth, a renewal, a reminder, a remembering, a transformation, which offers hope again and again in the hours, days, weeks, and months that follow. Such hope is not made real in the ordinary wishes we may have for ourselves; it is both the action and the end result, emerging because of the eternal possibility of enduring life, of hope. We are all *held* in resurrection. From beginning to end, from start to finish, our individual lives and what we do with them are themselves witnesses to the existence of hope.

In this section we look at what witnessing might mean and how we can bring it to the front of our lives, taking it forward in practical ways.

To begin with, we must witness the void, the emptiness in which hope might be created and the space in which it might thrive, in order to realize that something can come to life there and then lead us forward. We can gaze into this void, perhaps without necessarily finding anything – at first. But we must keep going. This might seem pointless, delusional, but we have to hold on in faith, knowing that something might soon drop, unbidden, into the empty space. This is to stare at the empty white page or the blank canvas, knowing that words or paint will surely soon come to fill it, even though for the moment we don't know what our creative process will fashion into reality. We then need to stir our cauldron of thoughts, experiences, ideas, changing things around, putting things together, then separating them again. Words must be tasted, juxtaposed, pulled apart and their order changed. Some must be discarded so that others can reach the air and flourish. Ingredients need mixing and testing, ideas need to be sketched out first and experimented with – perhaps then abandoned, to be used another time. Magic is in the air. There are unexpected discoveries – things may have been lying dormant for a very long time and now is their moment to come into the Light.

In witnessing or "bearing witness" perhaps we are the eyes of God. We do it not on our own behalf, but on behalf of everything that is. We are not ourselves, or acting as ourselves, but on behalf of the "other," which lies behind everything. From this inner witnessing, prompted by the inner guide, we build up layer upon layer of inner, inward knowing. Or we plunge deeper and deeper into the depths of knowing, gradually leaving the uneasy sense of not-knowing behind. The scales begin to fall away. This idea might be hard to get hold of, but it is not for us to try to comprehend it. There is no need for such work. We have only to release ourselves from the pressure of understanding and just to witness, to know deeply. In the spirit of searching and witnessing we can find great openings, but if we are closed off and resistant to exploration then nothing can change.

We also need to witness both light and dark aspects of life, plus the shades in between – extremes and their variants have to co-exist, or richness and diversity may be absent. Life is not as it should or could be. Dark and light aren't fully realized without the opposite. The contrast points up the difference, the dynamism; the way the two fight each other, exist side by side amicably or glance off each other. Contrast brings them alive, setting them against each other. So we have to allow for both hope and despair to co-exist. Hope can be so very fragile. It is the candle puffed out by a gust of wind or a breath. But if we lose track of hope we can be sure that it will become a living thing again, automatically, before too long. Optimism is one of our natural human states and an unbidden upward boost will surely happen eventually. So to search without knowing must be a major part of the witnessing process and therefore of the possibility of searching for, and finding, the living hope.

Having a gap, a pause, a void, a space, a cauldron may seem to be the natural result of not being able to find the slip-road onto the more positive highway. But it is a good place and can yield great things. It may be at the center of all that is, a magical space into which things can move, find air and space, ideas and inspiration, stimulation and growth, acquiring new life in the process, or it may be a mixing bowl in which ingredients can be combined and a result emerge. The empty cauldron is the place for our creativity, where we can stir and produce something new. It is unpredictable in the sense of not knowing what will happen, because something else is at work, and it is a great way of witnessing the void deeply. It is capacious, with enough room for vigorous mixing, adding air. Chemistry can be facilitated. There is room to move. The very act of mixing and stirring is mindful, contemplative, and produces ideas in itself. It is also transformative, moving us on in hope.

Sometimes there are discussions about Quaker meetings, whether it is good to have a table in the center of the worshiping space, the circle of chairs. If there is one, it may be laden with books, which can feel overwhelming: Bibles, copies of *Quaker Faith and Practice, Advices and Queries* and others. It is as though there is essential knowledge to be found between these covers, which there is, but is the wrong emphasis placed on them by positioning them so centrally? There may also be a small vase of flowers in the center. Perhaps, mistakenly, this can make it seem like an altar. It is all too easy to keep focusing on it – whether at the books or flowers or just the reflections and colors. Perhaps it would be better to have an empty space – a void – instead, which could hold us together as a single entity more easily. This might be like staring into a deep well – the floor would melt away, with no bottom. We would imagine what is down there and possibility might come up from the empty space.

Wherever you are, wherever you go, discovery is a potential in an empty space, especially if you are a reluctant traveler or the way looks difficult. There is learning to be had. The places that offer the greatest physical challenge may offer the greatest teachings. At a Buddhist temple, far away, are seventy-two stupas, housing seated Buddhas. There are glimpses of quiet faces through stone tracery. But the topmost one is empty. It is a void. It takes a long time to walk up the outside, which is like a mountain, in the heat. The place is popular. It is best to start early, while the day is young and cool. The layout is a mandala and the route is circular, gradually working upward through different layers of awareness, in a state of meditation, all the time fighting physical challenges. The topmost empty stupa is a reminder of the void – of the emptiness of looking within and the self-sufficiency of the empty center. We all confront our own voids, within and without. The idea of working upward is to gradually become aware of something, to discover the void within self and to find meaning there. Perhaps the point of going there is to notice how we are feeling as we climb and then reflect afterward. Heat, thirst, fatigue, wonder, ignorance, mystification, discovery add to the mix. Meaning may come in a rush, in the moment, or it may emerge later.

We do not have to travel or go far to look into our cauldrons and see the void waiting to be filled. We can stop activity, sit in meditation and go within, to nothingness. Something will want to enter that space, so it will not remain empty for long.

The questions that follow are about how we "see," or don't "see," life as fully as we might, about how we witness. Are we noticing what really needs to be noticed? Are we absorbing the information, or do our overactive minds sometimes cut us off from whatever it is we most need? How and what are we witnessing? The questions are accompanied by short stories from real life, to act as examples and inspiration, and by practical exercises. Choose the ones that speak to you – and go slowly.

Questions about witnessing

Question: How well do we witness ourselves and our own lives? How well do we "take heed to the promptings of love and truth (*Advices and Queries* 1)"? And how well do we take heed of inner promptings to act in the world? How well do we really witness and know ourselves? From a place of witness and knowledge about the self, we can try to witness and know others and move into hopeful creativity and action. From a place of having more hope ourselves, we might be able to bring hope to others. The quote from *Advices and Queries* above asks us to listen to inner promptings, which call us to action through love and truth. From a place of witnessing and recognizing ourselves a little bit more, we can listen to a positive voice within that makes suggestions about how we might act in the world. This is the voice of hope and it asks us to dive into our self-knowledge, thereby strengthening it, building on the hope already present, layer added to layer.

Story: The party
It's good to give people the benefit of the doubt and refrain from making assumptions. Is the fault more on their side or on ours? Could making the effort to witness the self bring self-knowledge in order to avoid apportioning blame?

★ ★ ★

The couple were on their way to a party. It was at the invitation of an old friend. Some of the group hadn't seen each other for several decades, so it would be an emotional, joyful occasion. The drive went smoothly enough, but a friend they had given a lift to was causing upset.

They had wanted to make a new start, but had forgotten how annoying this friend had been in the past; it seemed she hadn't changed much. It all came flooding back. Unbelievably self-involved, she spent the entire journey with her head wedged between the two front-seat headrests, talking about her life in enormous detail. Any attempt at normal exchange was quickly diverted into further detail about herself. There was no escape.

By the time they arrived, exhaustion had set in. The same happened on the return journey.

During the weekend, one annoying episode piled on another. She was late, made demands, was fussy about food and generally self-centered. This all brought back times gone by.

They had wanted to give her a second chance, to wipe the slate clean, start again, but had discovered, too late, that nothing had changed. In fact, things seemed worse. Or were they? Could some of the fault, at the very least, lie on the other side? A while later, they wondered how the friend had felt about the weekend and about them. Did they annoy her as much as she had annoyed them? Did they push her buttons too?

Activity: Going within

This basic centering exercise can guide us within, in order to begin to search and witness the self better. Going within can, at the very least, help us become aware of all the things that upset us and all the things that might calm us.

Start by asking why things upset or calm you. When you feel upset, bring to mind everything that might be able to help you. Think of simple things that you can pull out of your first-aid kit whenever needed. Knowing exactly what makes you worry, causes you distress is the first step toward being able to help yourself and allay that worry. You can't stop the worry until you know what triggers it. And until you know what can help you, you can't move forward to a healthier state of mind. Self-knowledge is the key. You may have to summon bravery if you start delving and don't like what you find. It may be hard to face the less pleasant things, but these are part of you too, of course.

- Sit comfortably and close your eyes or adopt a soft gaze. Silence any distractions. Hold on to the aim of emptying your mind.
- Pause all your everyday thoughts as far as you can.

19

- Go within, reaching inward toward your deepest center.
- Find the place where everything is perfectly still. Perhaps everything else spins around it.
- Stay in this place as long as you can, until you have explored it fully.
- Emerge from this state and open your eyes again.
- Move forward with your day.

Question: How do we witness our lives' purposes?

Finding one's own truth is about pulling all of oneself into single focus – one entity rather than a collection of different features and attributes. It means including failures as well as successes, ups as well as downs, weaknesses as well as strengths. As the quote (p. xi) invites, we are asked to concentrate all aspects of ourselves into one strength, one energy, finding more meaning and purpose in so doing. Thus, one can find life purpose and discern what we are here for. Then we can move forward with intention – with hope.

After a while, there must be a time of reckoning, of weighing up, of assessing. Many things have been done, tried out, succeeded at, failed at or abandoned, but are they really what we are meant to be doing? We have only one life. What really makes us tick? Have we chosen the easier routes when harder ones would have taught us more? Have we made a habit of avoiding difficulty? Could we have challenged ourselves more than we have? Or could we have given ourselves an easier time, perhaps? A good starting point might be looking at what we noticed about ourselves when we were young.

What is present in life as it is? What could we do that we are not doing? What changes could we make? How could we look at things and see them in a different light? We delve as deeply as we can, reaching a point of inner stillness, perhaps. We pause restless thinking, all feelings of dissatisfaction, all questing, restless searching, all that seems unsatisfying. We contemplate all the things that satisfy us deeply, which make us feel complete, contented, which we want to do whenever we can. We think about which activities make us feel more ourselves. We can also think about the things that perhaps we have not done but always felt we wanted to try. Perhaps we have been funneled, or have funneled ourselves, down one particular route, ignoring or forgetting about other possibilities, a choice, taken years earlier, when still unformed, may have now taken over most of life. We can try accessing ourselves as children and think about the things we felt drawn to then. Have we continued to explore these in our lives since then?

Story: A child of eight
A child explores, is gradually drawn out by a skilled teacher, and witnesses part of herself in the process.

★ ★ ★

A child of eight or nine sat at a tiny desk, twisting her left hand awkwardly, trying to avoid pencil clashes with her right-handed friend. This sometimes made her feel odd, different. As her teacher stood at the front of the room, speaking, explaining or reading, the girl could hear poetry in her voice, the beauty of the words, the sense, the passion and the music, the cadence. It was inspiring. Everything seemed to fall into place; it made sense and had meaning, even the boring parts or those she couldn't understand. She felt confident that she soon would understand. The teacher was kind and encouraging, but serious, without a scrap of humor. She took the children seriously and treated them as though they were older than they were. This made the children feel good about themselves. The words were cohesive and rhythmical. Mysteries, such as punctuation marks and parts of speech, were audible and therefore had a purpose, a reason for being. They made the words hang together and take on added richness. Words felt easy, light, and straightforward. Hanging together, they made perfect sense, flowing out of the child, through her awkward left hand, onto the paper. The ideas were unstoppable, holding their own energy, like a stream. Writing them down brought them to life and light.

Activity: Writing from the heart

Take the first idea that comes to mind and just start writing. Without thinking. No need to agonize or plan. No need to sit and stare at the blank page or screen without inspiration. Writing from the heart loosens inhibitions about putting pen to paper and it gets creative juices flowing. One idea leads to another and before long, ideas are piling in and spilling over each other, desperate to find a home in the world, on paper, noticed and heard. This activity, in itself, seems to access the unconscious mind, the part that just carries on working, turning over, all by itself.

- Start a new file or open a new page. Choose whatever tools and equipment that you enjoy using. Take care over choice of pens and pencils, as the process of physically writing must give you joy and not be a struggle.
- Take a random word or phrase that pops into your head, without filtering or questioning. This is your jumping-off point. See what flows from here.
- Without further thought, just write whatever comes to you, in the moment. Let ideas feed into each other. Don't edit or revise what you write at this stage, just write and see what happens, keeping an open mind and heart. Don't be embarrassed about what you write – no one is going to read it but you.
- After about ten minutes, stop and re-read, without changing anything. What you read may surprise you.

Ideas that you might have been unaware of may have emerged. You may find that you write in order to discover rather than to set down what you already know. This may be a revelation.

- Try doing the same every day for a while. You may find that it loosens up your creativity in many different ways.

Question: How do we witness others?

How well do we really know someone? Have we been misreading the signs? Is this related to how well we know, or do not know, ourselves? Have we been judgmental when we could, or should, have just let things be? Let that person be? Was our way any better or was it just different? Listening is part of witnessing. It may be much easier to witness whatever is in others' lives than in one's own. It is all too easy to feel that we "know" what the facts are. We may well build up a mistaken picture. But the inner judge has to be firmly kept under control. However, reflection on the lives of others can lead us further into witnessing our own lives, and then we can make changes there.

Story: The Achilles Heel

The business of knowing others starts off with our first awareness of getting to know our parents, especially mothers. This is all part of our early witness of life. In this case, the child thought she witnessed perfection and strength, and the exposure of weakness was a surprising revelation.

★★★

The mother was an independent person. Self-possessed; in charge of her own realm. She knew what she wanted, always, and usually she just went ahead and did it. People admired her for this strength. No one could push her around and she stood up for herself. She could take risks, though she could be cautious too. This was the 1950s and middle-class married women were housewives. None of her friends worked or had careers. All that came to a halt the moment the ring was on the finger. But she enjoyed being in charge of the domestic side of life. Practical and capable, she could do anything with aplomb, expertly, taking great satisfaction in it.

One day she made the decision to go back to work, feeling the pull of something beyond the domestic sphere. She had hardly experienced much of a working life before marriage and she felt the lack of it. She quickly found herself a part-time post, bought her own car and planned life like a neatly fitting jigsaw. The father supported her, though probably without quite realizing how the seamless operation that was his home really ran. She made it look so easy.

One day the mother was negotiating her car gingerly along a country lane between high, dense hedges. Her driving style was, mystifyingly, quite different from the father's calm, smooth vehicle-handling. It didn't reflect her, either, because it was far from confident. The children were wedged tightly in the back seat beside a stack of trays full of ripe soft fruit. The mother was going to make jam. Without warning she started gesticulating toward an opening in a hedge, where a combine harvester was working. With only one hand on the wheel and looking to one side, she somehow lost control and the car swerved into the ditch, coming to rest at a sharp angle. The children found themselves squashed to one side, at a steep slant, covered in crushed fruit. Clothes were stained red, though thankfully no blood had been spilled. The mother had let her guard drop, for the first time ever, it seemed. This perfect person had revealed herself to be less than perfect and this became part of the child's early life-witness, her experience. For a while the child was shaken, perturbed, but later this became a learning about her witness of others, who may not be perfect, as none of us are.

Activity: Try positive people-watching

Sometimes you have to wait, in a public place, with nothing to do. Perhaps you fall into the habit of looking at other people. When you look at people, those you don't know, do you judge as an automatic response? It is easy to have a tape running in your head that is always judgmental and negative: "wrong glasses," "bad colors," "bad clothes choice" – the list goes on. The next time this happens, change negative thoughts into positives: "great hair," "lovely face," "great colors," "nice bag" and see how different this makes you feel. Appreciate everyone you see for their individuality and what they bring. Suddenly the world is a better place, more hopeful.

Question: How can we witness boredom as a place of potential?
What do we do in odd, empty moments? Or, at least, in moments that seem empty. Do we feel anxious when they occur? Do we feel guilty about not doing anything? Do we rush to fill the seeming emptiness? Can we sit, instead, with witnessing this emptiness? Just accepting it and letting it be. Perhaps this is an opportunity for witnessing meaning when there seems to be none, witnessing something where there seems to be nothing? An act of creativity may leap in to fill such a void. But feeling the void is something that has to be witnessed in life. Think of this as a chance for your mind to rest and recuperate. Your mind needs to feel empty in order to move ahead in thought once more.

Story: A new life

Sometimes having something removed from your life and witnessing an emptiness makes you appreciate what remains more intensely. A point of boredom may allow you to look within.

★ ★ ★

The friends met regularly for outings. They had fun and could find something interesting to say about almost anything. Feelings of boredom and depression could be conquered for half a day. At the end of a third lockdown they were prone to mood swings, unexplained ups and downs, so finding positives in life seemed to be more important than ever.

The shopping center was a gap-toothed crone, forgotten, decaying, ignored. Some shops were shuttered forever; others might open again, one day. The women wondered how they would look back on this moment in the future, when things were "back to normal." They felt desperate. They peered at sad window displays, gathering dust. Christmas trees in March. A one-way walking policy, with loud arrows telling them which way to go, directed them without mercy. This seemed quite unnecessary as there was no one else there. There was nowhere to sit since all the seats had been removed. They marched around the two floors, glancing quickly to either side. Here lay forgotten dreams. However, two large shops remained open, like friendly lighthouses. The friends felt the magnetic draw toward light and life and prowled the aisles, inspecting merchandise. They discussed the merits and demerits of many different items, and all the anecdotes they prompted. Temptation was everywhere, but they did not need or want any of it. They didn't buy. They could not and did not want to. Nothing new was needed in their new pared-down lives; the idea of choosing seemed unfamiliar, a long-forgotten skill. It confused them, made them indecisive. The bright colors were overwhelming. They had thought they wanted things, but they found that they did not. A moment of needing to find something outwardly had allowed them to witness a place of boredom within, perhaps finding something different there.

Activity: Stare at your blank canvas

All new artworks have to start with a blank canvas, and a relaxed, centered mind before a spark can ignite. An idea can inhabit the empty space and something can start to take shape, evolve – a new creation can come into being. There has to be "nothing" before "something" can emerge and take shape. If you witness nothing, you may feel a sense of panic, though you know that you have to do something. Whether you have a deadline or just a deep-felt need to create, or experience a feeling that something needs to be born, the sensation may be the same. There seems to be nothing at first, but something will surely take its place, even if it takes a while.

- Clear your space, minimize distractions, so that you can sweep the way clean in front of you and be left facing yourself rather than perhaps absorbing other people's ideas.
- Then listen and hear from your own center and take confidence in knowing that whatever comes up is for you to explore further, as you see fit.
- Stare at your blank canvas or your blank page, without a time limit.
- Start to paint or write, or whatever activity you are engaged in, without thinking.
- If nothing happens at first, try again another time.

Question: Can witnessing be doing nothing at all?
Idle, seemingly unproductive, moments of waiting for the next thing to happen may cause irritation, a feeling of time being lost or wasted, but they can be used and taken advantage of. Take this time to notice, really notice. What can emerge from this? Something good, positive, and charged with hope? These times can provide entertainment, amusement, bemusement, and be thought-provoking and inspirational. A creative idea might arrive as a result of this witness.

Story: The lesson in "wasting" time

There was a time when children were urged to fill every minute, otherwise it was seen as "wasted" time, never to be returned. Every moment was to be used wisely, productively. However, this idea now seems meaningless. A moment may not be "productive" in the accepted way, but idle time can be used creatively, without knowing exactly how or what the long-term effects might be. All thoughts and actions seem to go into the pot, the cauldron, in which magic may, or may not, happen. This may not occur straight away, but be pulled out later, when the time is right.

★ ★ ★

A very old woman stood at the front of the class. She seemed far too old to be allowed to teach, possibly even to be alive at all. The children had never seen her smile or utter anything cheerful, though she must have had a lighter side – they sometimes heard other teachers call her by an affectionate, amusing nickname. She had carefully curled white hair arranged in a barely-there hairnet and she sported a restrained row of tiny pearls. She came to the school once a week, taught scripture and then disappeared again. She always carried a heavy leather bag with a large clasp, which she opened and closed with great solemnity, taking out a small leather-cased traveling clock when she needed to check the time. The children observed her every move, mannerism, flicker of life, with fascination. One day, she left the classroom saying she would be back "soon." The children were unexpectedly left to their own devices, with no instructions. They soon started playing about, as children will, making a noise. Time went by and the teacher still did not return. Suddenly the door burst open and in she strode, a picture of blustering rage. She shouted, telling them in no uncertain terms what she thought of them. The phrase that stuck with them was the guilt-provoking: "You will never get back those wasted minutes."

Activity: Stare into space

Children are sometimes told, or made to feel, that just staring into space is a bad idea. They are discouraged from doing it – especially if they are supposed to be paying attention to something or somebody. So we all grow up feeling that staring into space is wasteful, lacking meaning and purpose – that we ought to be doing something. We feel guilt, not positivity, when we find ourselves taking a moment out from busy-ness.

This exercise is about helping us find witness to let go of the activity of the mind. The eyes go into soft focus and are rested, the body and mind relax, without clear direction, and ideas are born.

- Sit comfortably, relax, gaze into the distance, allowing your eyes to shift to soft focus.
- Let go of your everyday thoughts, all the concerns, worries, "to-do lists," monkey-mind activity, all the surface activity of daily life.
- Allow your mind to float wherever it wants to go.
- Stay in this free-moving place for about ten minutes, if possible.
- Return to normal focus and awareness, and your day.
- Later, notice whether any fresh thoughts or ideas occurred to you.
- Perhaps make a habit of this practice before you embark on any creative endeavor or any other action that requires your full-focus witness and inward spirit.

Question: Is witnessing life's magic possible?

Finding something that's a little magical about everyday life can bring hope rushing back in to the places where it has been lost or hiding. Just a simple awareness of this as a possibility can make hope feel a lot nearer than before, bringing a different "smell" to life. The feeling may arrive unbidden and unlooked-for, when least expected, bringing a rush of energy and positivity in its wake. Anything may now seem possible, when a few minutes before it was not.

Story: Witnessing magic

Magic can be a certain way of witnessing life; seeing a different side, a new perspective, aspect, dimension. Sometimes it is easily witnessed, but sometimes it is just not there that day. But this day turned out to be a magic day.

★ ★ ★

The friends went for a walk. They were both tired – not on top form. A walk did not seem quite welcome, but they knew that soon they would see a return of good spirits. Putting one foot in front of the other would do its work – magic would kick in. They walked up paths and down slopes. There was mud everywhere in wide, sticky tracts. There were people and dogs in colorful coats. The weather was damp, overcast. They stared at trees. There was a soft cast to the light and the colors seemed misty, muted, subtle. The branches formed stark shapes, interlacing tracery. They pointed out shapes and colors of leaves to each other, how they complemented each other and fitted together. Clusters of red berries stood out as splashes of brightness which forced them to gaze, and gaze again. The air was still. They took their time, relishing views and angles. Things normally ignored, or only briefly glanced at, were dwelled on at length, commented on in every possible detail. They had the urge to squeeze more and more juice out of the fruit of the experience of being there, in that moment, on that day. There was plenty of time – no need to rush, nothing else happening. Everything seemed fresh and new, as if seen for the first time.

Later they found the coffee place. It was like an oasis in a desert. It was surreal: empty. Sustenance allowed the friends more positivity: they noticed an empty bench facing a green unpeopled expanse, a cheerful man renovating a rubbish bin, a notice displaying bad grammar. They then started on a verbal demolition of a politician, a member of the Royal family, a fresh binge-watch, an untried page-turner, an adventurous way of using Alexa, a good shampoo for thinning hair, walking boots for repelling mud, recent weird dreams – the topics flowed endlessly and seemed fascinating. They were accessing a side of life that usually remains beneath the surface, ignored, or considered too mundane to bother about. They seemed to be witnessing more and enjoying the seemingly trivial more than usual. The magic of its simplicity now seemed so obvious. Why had it taken all this time to be able to see it?

<u>Activity: Look at a leaf</u>
Find something everyday, simple, and really look at it. See if there are qualities that you have missed before or have not had time to look at.

- Find a leaf that appeals to the "you-ness" of you. It is special and it stands out from all the others. There is no other leaf quite like it and it seems to attract you – it is different and it draws you in.
- Spend as long as you want to, or need to, looking at the leaf. Become aware of all its aspects: shape, colors, textures, blemishes, hairs – and any other details your eye finds. Use a magnifier if you want to.
- Contemplate what it is about this leaf that attracts you and think about why that might be.
- Is there anything to learn? Perhaps the way you look at things normally is too glancing, not contemplative enough, and you could spend longer exploring this way of seeing.

Question: How can our witness turn negatives into positives?
Looking on the bright side may seem an annoying and trite way to witness life. It is impossible to achieve – or only sometimes. The phone keeps announcing another communication. It is grating on the nerves. Switch to silent? The posts are not intended for you, they are between other friends, old childhood friends, good friends. Their topic for discussion is not of interest to you, but it is good to know that they are enjoying themselves, exchanging jokes. They are there – after all this time. This is reassuring.

<u>Story: The museum</u>
Some buildings are designed to convey an integral message, which you may only witness subliminally, or the memory of its meaning may only surface later. Challenging at the time, perhaps, later it will add significance and depth to the visit.

★★★

The museum was hard work. The corridor sloped downward, which was easy, though surprising. After a while the visitors noticed that the incline went the other way – upward. They now had to put far more effort into walking. It was hard work. Legs started to feel heavy, breathing too. The architecture conveyed its own message physically. Display cases demanded attention, making the visitors stop to look and read. They felt disturbed. Three rooms, named "voids," formed focal points in the building. The visitors moved further inward, but the way was unclear, labyrinthine. They had to move slowly, without being aware of direction or having the ability to influence it. There were no choices on offer. The inclines became steeper and steeper. The visitors were doing what the architect forced them to do and they were beginning to suffer. There was no other way – no alternative route. They just had to endure.

In the distance, a long way away, they could hear a clinking sound, like chains or gravel being crunched underfoot. Soon they had to walk across loose metal faces, which were wearing different expressions, some smiling, some laughing, some with downturned, despairing expressions, all shapes and sizes. Treading right on them was difficult to do, but necessary to get to the other side. The visitors flinched. They trampled on others, as though making them suffer, furthering selfish ends, to get what they wanted. The visitors looked up and found themselves at the bottom of one of the voids – the ceiling was high, dark, hardly visible. It was gloomy and far away. Perhaps there was a message about noticing, thinking, being, experiencing, learning – witnessing.

<u>Activity: Giving as witnessing</u>
Try practicing a meditation of thanks, for anything or anyone important to you, using a personal mantra. This is a form of witness, an acknowledgment of the feeling of gratefulness. This could be as simple as repeating "thanks" to yourself, to the universe, but it is meaningful to you in the most heart-felt way possible, in that brief moment. When you use this as your special word, repeat it in the deepest part of you and witness it inwardly. The key is to witness thanks completely and utterly, so wait for the right moment.

- Settle your thoughts, wherever you are.
- Go inward to find your deepest self.
- Breathe in and out, evenly.
- After a while, draw your focus toward the word "thanks" and let that take over your mind and heart.
- Shift the focus of your thanks to the recipient of them, or toward the nature or purpose of them.
- Rest within your thanks for as long as you feel you need to.

Question: Can we witness "nothings" turning into "somethings"?
Sometimes it is good to witness and harness a random, passing thought and turn it into a "something." Otherwise it just drifts away and has only transient meaning, which may soon be dismissed and forgotten. Try witnessing all the small, seemingly insignificant, things in life as having meaning, and therefore hope. They can all add up to something and be of consequence.

Story: The book with the red cover
Synchronicity can be a "nothing" or a "something." It probably depends on mood. It can be dismissed as a chance coming together, a coincidence, or it can be layered up with clothes of significance. If there is the need, it can be witnessed as a glimpse of hope.

★ ★ ★

An old photograph arrived on her phone. It had been taken several decades before. The woman did not immediately recognize herself, but eventually she saw that the girl reading a hardback book with a red cover was, in fact, her, but in a former life. That world seemed like another world. Only the book linked today with that time. It was still in her possession, sitting on her bookshelf now, in this very room. She only had to glance up to see it to receive a jolt of recognition, synchronicity. Everything else was different, unrecognizable: people, place, hair, body, clothes. But that very book was in front of the woman now, in the present. It was a bit worn and scuffed, the dust jacket torn and peeling, the corners dented. Inside there were margin scrawlings, handwriting unrecognizable. Did she really write that? Were those her thoughts? The book was battered, yellowed, but the content was the same, unchanged. The coincidence, the book's enduring presence in her life, seeing it on her shelf just at the moment of looking at the photograph, seemed to offer a moment of meaning.

Activity: Treasure old things

Take the time to look at some old treasures; things that come from an earlier part of life but which do not re-summon pain or negativity. Such things may have been part of your life for a long time and you may not even really see them any more, since they are so familiar and so much part of your life. Think of the person you once were and who you are now. Think of all the years in between and all the things that have happened; all the changes that have taken place. This may be part of witnessing hope in life.

Question: Can we witness by slowing down and savoring?

Avoid rushing so much, which can lead to a life of "getting things done," living in the future, regretting past actions. Witness, savor, and enjoy the present. Make the most of it. Look around. Perhaps sometimes circumstances force us to slow down and witness the world properly.

Story: The exhibition

An art exhibition gives the ideal chance to witness in terms of looking, really looking. But it has to be given time and attention. The eyes must go soft and move around the piece without disturbance. Other distractions have to be minimized and eliminated, if possible. Concentration has to be maintained and a flow state of looking discovered within. Afterward it will be possible to witness the art again at will, in the mind's eye.

★ ★ ★

The woman went to an exhibition. She experienced a huge sense of freedom. It was exciting. She found herself moving quickly across empty floors, which were like great empty skating rinks. No one else was there, only the occasional attendant. The pictures were huge, vast, resplendent in their glory. They sang out, telling their stories, unimpeded by anything. Each one announced itself in its unique way. The frames shone, glowed, contrasting with the gorgeous colors that had been carefully selected for the walls, the palette chosen to chime with the artist's own choices. Vast acreages of autumnal tones, changing from one room to the next, contrasting and complementing. Themes changed. No one else was there to block the view of the low-hung paintings. No phones held high, no distracting conversations. No queuing, picture by picture, waiting for someone to shuffle to the next one. No waiting for a space on the seat to rest. The paintings seemed three-dimensional, tactile, full of movement, considered and precise, flowing and dynamic. It was an opportunity to relax, drink in, and truly witness.

Activity: Witness colors in the world

Rather than witnessing with your "brain," witness with your heart. Look for colors that sing out to you rather than searching for subject and meaning. Leave content and subject-matter aside.

- Look for color contrasts, matching and complementary colors. These could be in nature or the man-made world. Sometimes colors are accidental – perhaps the result of rusting or decay. There are rich colors in rotting fruit just as in a perfect display of ripe fruit.
- Dwell on color for as long as you can – perhaps even a whole day – avoiding seeing shape, texture, or form, as you might normally do.
- See how individual shades affect you emotionally.
- Contemplate how this has changed the way you now look at things.

Activity: Witness shapes around you

Sometimes we may need tools or a project to help us to slow down. Looking at the world in terms of shape may be a good way of slowing down.

- Just for one day, try to see the world in terms of the shapes of objects that are everywhere, rather than their sense, meaning, purpose. This will have the effect of slowing you down and changing the way you approach life.
- See angles, curves, interlocking forms, and the way they bounce off each other, complement each other or fight each other.
- Witness and enjoy all the various shapes that abound everywhere.

Chapter 2

Living

[T]here will ye witness a living Hope.
Margaret Fell

Are we living or are we existing? Are we in charge of life, or is life in charge of us? Do we live to work or work to live? What does it mean to "live"? If we are truly to "live," living must mean "living in Immanence" in order to have meaning. It is to be fully present in life and then to voice something and to bring out into the open that which is within (which has surely been coaxed into being through having been "witnessed"). Life is to fully "be." It is about accessing the depths and sensing the presence of "other." It is also about accessing personal creativity. Imagery is a useful tool in the understanding of this, but it can also get in the way, impeding, real, useful vision. Creativity and immanence are connected – or are they the same thing? Perhaps so, since both can lead to transformation and transcendence. But how can we live in immanence, living in the now? To "live" is to fully experience life and to live in hope is the only way to get there. Without being propelled by the upward force of hope life starts to dwindle, to drift sideways, then away. Hope has to be kept alive and vibrant, a "living" hope – otherwise it is not hope at all, it cannot thrive, so it dies.

Hope is all about living with faith, the energy that drives life, and then holding on to it, having the faith to move forward, driving energy upward in the sure and certain knowledge that all will come right in the end. This is to have faith in hope and from that place to hope to have faith within, in the very center. This is the Light within, the focus of life and hope.

We can ask ourselves about whether we can really enhance the "living" part of who we are, to fathom out who we are and how we live, thinking about ways we can live more fully to witness the hope and the faith. Perhaps we are not already living life to the full, and what our lives are for, as much as we might. Perhaps we are holding ourselves back in ways we are not fully aware of, or are only dimly glimpsing. These ways may be passing beneath our deepest awareness because they are about how we have been raised, our personalities and our conditionings. Is there more to tease out in our experience of how we live, so that we might live more fully?

The aging process can hold us back from living our best lives, as we are, now. Confidence may dwindle and the easiest, most comfortable, route might be relaxed into, thereby missing out on the life that is still there to be lived with a bit of effort, health being good. But this can be reversed. For example, a woman was preparing for a gig. The scene was a muddle of flexes and bits of tape, instruments, electronic equipment and music stands. There was a distinct danger of tripping and falling over. The air was full of tuning and adjustments, and anticipation. All the musicians with her were of a certain age and you could taste the wealth of experience gathered there, all in one place. The woman had great style. She was in the now and owned it too. "Cool" was a word that could have been invented for her. Her long gray hair was swept behind one ear to reveal a complicated long earring, which caught the light. She wore an elegant bargee's cap, sporting shining silver rivets on either side. Many bracelets and rings adorned her wrists and hands and a bomber jacket with skinny jeans and elegant boots completed her look. The small trappings of her craft, such as plectrums and capos, were kept in a little black velvet bag, which she laid carefully at her feet on the stage. What followed was "living"; a coming together of many elements to create something vibrant and alive.

It was a witness to life lived and life to come, to creativity and skill made manifest, leading to great hope in the moment.

The questions that follow are about how we "live," or don't "live" life as fully as we might. Are we witnessing what really needs to be witnessed in order that we might live more fully? The questions are supported by short stories from real life, to act as examples and inspiration, and by practical exercises. Choose the ones that speak to you – and go slowly.

Questions about living

Question: Can we live more by taking some risks?
This question is about the possibility of living in a spirit of outgoing adventurousness. It is easy to get into the habit of being risk averse and some of us are brought up to be this way. It comes with the territory of "being careful" and "staying safe" – particularly for girls and women, who are discouraged from being adventurous, unlike boys and men, for whom it is often the opposite. It's easy for some of us to always try to remain within a comfort zone rather than taking the harder road, and all the risks that might go with it. Uncomfortable and difficult situations seem unwelcome at the time, but afterward they are the very things that are remembered and passed down. Such incidents make funny and dramatic stories. The things that went "right," according to plan, seem anodyne, pedestrian by comparison and are soon forgotten.

Story: The race
This story is an example of a young person wanting to explore beyond her comfort zone and test herself in her life, but then wondering why she was doing it. Taking risks may pose such open questions about what it is to live and to be alive.

★★★

The girl was soaked to the skin, sailing a small boat in a storm. This was bad enough. But worse than that, she was in charge of two young children, who seemed to be hanging on for dear life, too frightened to speak. They did whatever she told them, grimly and unquestioningly. They trusted her. However, the teenager barely knew what she was doing, except that she had to survive and get the children home safely. She did not know why she had agreed to do this. Her answer, to herself, fell somewhere between pride, stubbornness, and needing to prove herself – or all three, though she could easily have just used the weather as an excuse for not going. No one would have blamed her. It was a race, but she was past caring about that. She had almost no competitive instinct at the best of times and she did not care who won or where she came in. She just needed to make it back in one piece. She followed the boat in front of her and replicated their maneuvers as exactly as she could. She put her trust in them, entirely. She looked down at her wet, slippery hands, gripping. Strands of hair whipped across her face. The waves were high. Again, she wondered what she was trying to prove, to herself, to anyone. She felt foolish because no one had forced her to do this. She had just decided to test herself and try out possibilities – bravery, adventurousness, competence. And now she regretted it, bitterly. She was aware that others had put their trust in her, but she had felt weak and pathetic at the time. It would have been better if she'd just admitted this to herself and left riskiness to others. Later, back on dry land, she found herself surrounded by relieved, beaming adults and even a warm glow of inner satisfaction. Perhaps it had been worth taking a risk after all. Decades later she realized that you have to take risks in order to grow and to live.

Activity: Take the harder option
The next time there is a choice of direction, take the harder option and see where it leads. Make the less-straightforward

choice. It could be more enriching, taking you out of your usual way. Before you embark, ask yourself the following questions:

- Is the choice new and different for you?
- Does it teach you anything? It may turn out to be far more interesting and memorable – and you may learn more from it long term.
- Did the choice wake you up in some way?
- Did it make you think about something differently or re-think something?
- Did it make you question something?

Question: Can we live more by being spontaneous?

This question is closely related to the preceding one (p. 40). It is about living more adventurously and being prepared to be in the moment more than usual. How much do we live in the moment rather than planning everything first? But perhaps having been open to something new and different, can we use discernment to assess it – and decide what our actions should be? Close planning comes naturally to the risk averse, automatically. Every moment is thought through, lived out in advance, even. This means that if nothing is left to chance, some unexpected things may be overlooked, ignored, and not taken advantage of. These things could have been life-enhancing, enriching, to be learned from.

Story: The drive

Taking a long trip on the spur of the moment may seem like madness to some but living adventurously to others. The aim is to see if it can be done and to test oneself when there could be easier options. However, the sense of satisfaction when it is all over makes it life-affirming and worthwhile.

★★★

On a whim, the woman decided to drive a long way to see a relative. The car was small and old, but it had recently passed its MOT, so she felt sure it was fine. It was easy to throw a few things into it, climb in and go rather than make complicated plans. There were two teenagers with her. Perhaps they could help find the way and provide moral support. After some miles of gray motorway, the woman realized that she might have bitten off more than she could chew. The teenagers were morose and self-absorbed. The only time they came to life was at a service station, where they consumed vast quantities of pricey food. They had no desire or will to learn how to read a map and didn't seem to care where they were going or how long it would take. The miles went by slowly and the way ahead seemed never-ending. After a while the woman's mind seemed to be playing tricks on her. Her hands could barely grip the wheel and decision-making about the route, as well as the rudiments of driving a car, were beginning to seem odd to her. She lost track of which gear she was in and the rules of the road, usually automatic, seemed strange and illogical. She was finding it hard to understand road signs and even remember which motorway she was on. Eventually she gave up trying to engage the teenagers in map-reading. She memorized the route and started to trust herself. A blast of confidence hit her and she experienced a rush of happiness. Soon they would arrive and all would be well. They stopped again for a quick snack and the soup was the best she had ever tasted. The countryside was beautiful and the roads were getting narrower. She found the way, arrived, and felt absurdly pleased with herself.

Activity: Get a (virtual) tattoo!

If you feel that your time for tattoos has been and gone, you could either ignore those thoughts and go ahead anyway, or you could keep the tattoo invisible, in your mind.

On a short course, all were invited to bring something with them. One person brought a virtual tattoo. It was written in her mind and she adopted the phrase for a while. The phrase was "Turn to the Light" and in her mind she had it tattooed on her inner wrist. Whenever she felt like it, she turned her wrist over and imagined seeing the words there. These words focused her and encouraged her in taking steps forward in life and living, in confidence. They were soothing, contemplative, reminding her of what she must do.

If a real tattoo is a step too far, and a virtual tattoo too forgettable, make a friendship bracelet from lettered beads instead.

Question: Can we live more by letting our wilder sides show?
The first thought is sometimes the best one, even if reviewing it later reveals something that seems a little odd when the cold light of day has been shone on it. But stick with the first idea because there was "something" there. The magical appearance of an idea is to be treasured. It's so easy for a good one to pop up, only to have the more rational, cautious thinking mind squash it with a cold blast of reservations and "what if" thoughts that may stem from lack of confidence and fear of judgment. Mistakes, if they really are mistakes, can be corrected later. Modifications can be made. If real mistakes cannot be corrected, then there is the chance to learn.

There may be a dream that reveals a "crazy" but "brilliant" idea. It is so good that it has the power to rouse from sleep. It is wise to write it down, as it may seem too outlandish in the morning since the rational side might stamp on it. All the most original, creative ideas seem over-the-top to begin with. But they are the ones that reveal the real and offer something new and interesting. Sometimes the sensible side reigns supreme, because this has been our schooling, learning, and teaching. It has been taken in and self-taught, sometimes for most of life, and the wild side never seems to get an outing. It's important to feel this other side come to life and live a bit. Know that it's not "crazy" but a vital part of the self that has been lying dormant. It is just as much a part of us as the more daily face and needs to come out. It is all part of the "God" within. An older person need not feel that this is not appropriate. A lifetime of experience gives the edge in almost any creative endeavor and can bring to life things that must not be dismissed. They will bring light and life to others.

Story: Flowers talking to each other
Sometimes a time of learning and discussion can open you up to a new vision, a new way of seeing, giving life a new "smell." The course, session, or conversation has awakened some hidden or forgotten part of life, which is now seen through new eyes.

★ ★ ★

The course had been stimulating, perhaps over-stimulating. The participants seemed bright-eyed but jangled and rattled. Their sensitivities had been prodded and poked. Some people were in tears, some were angry and talking loudly, some were laughing or just talking earnestly. Glancing toward the stove, the woman's eye snagged on a fresh flower arrangement. The blooms and foliage were a perfection of harmony, thought, creativity, care, love, skill – everything. All was visible in the one. The colors blended and complemented each other, an offering of the season from the garden. Looking more closely, she could see further subtleties. The shapes fitted into each other, the petals and leaves a perfectly intersecting jigsaw of curves and points. The flower heads resembled human heads, nodding sympathetically to each other. Different sizes formed family groups: mothers and daughters, fathers and sons. Grandparents. All looked toward each other in sympathy and understanding, having gentle conversations, chatting, making casual observations, passing the time of day. They seemed to reflect the wider world, the whole of life, in gentleness and kindness, giving a snapshot of how we might be and how we could be; how all could happily coexist. The next minute, the woman snapped into the present moment. Had she been asleep on her feet? Dreaming? Hallucinating? No, something had been unlocked – another way of seeing, a touch of creative vision had been released somehow. She took a picture of the flowers and went home. A while later she looked at the photo. All she saw was a nice bunch of flowers arranged in a tasteful vase, sitting on a stove. Beautiful but not exceptional, but somehow lacking the qualities she had seen in them before. She had returned to normal life.

Activity: What is your "wild side"?
What is your "wild side" and where can it lead you in life? Delve within. It might mean doing something you never imagined you could attempt, or going somewhere alone that you never felt brave enough to do. Or it could be trying to develop a side of yourself that has been on the back burner for years and never fully explored. Or it could be something you have dismissed as not being "you." Whatever it is:

- Try to sit with an idea that seems a bit crazy and then, rather than dismissing it, develop it further.
- Hold it and feel its pull, its power, its seduction.
- Think about why you are attracted to it and why it holds your imagination. This might even just be a small thing, but it accesses a different part of you, which you might not be used to, and perhaps it brings a new way of looking at the world and living in it, for you.
- If you can, push through and carry your wild idea into reality.

Question: Do we live in the present?

Are our thoughts constantly looking backward in time, or forward, or both? Are they ever relishing the "now"? We are so used to learning from the past and planning the future that sometimes the present can be completely forgotten. Accessing stillness and harnessing that feeling might help with this.

<u>Story: The moment of stillness</u>
Take a moment to truly live in the "now," with no past and no present, especially in difficult times.

★ ★ ★

The group had been experiencing great turbulence. There had been upset, threats, and recriminations. Many were trying to resolve the situation and meetings had been held to try to decide what to do. There was a residual state of shock, not to mention the feeling that what had been a time of peace had been destroyed – ruined beyond repair. The injustice of that was anger-inducing. The next mealtime found the woman sitting with some different people, who she had never met before. Gentle friendly chat with an older woman and a young mother and her baby restored equilibrium and she calmed down. Suddenly the older woman offered to hold the baby while the mother ate her meal. As the pair settled the woman noticed how practiced and capable the older woman was and the weight of the day seemed to lift. The pair seemed to be held in the palms of the Creator. They were sheltered, protected. They were everything that had ever been, and ever will be. A perfection bonded by love. The feeling of connection spread out into the room. There was trust, truth, bliss – all held together in that moment – in the woman's adoring gaze at the child's sleeping face. Hope in life and in living was restored in that moment of stillness.

Activity: Living in stillness
Take a few moments to live in stillness in daily life.

- Sit comfortably and close your eyes or adopt a soft gaze. If you are out, try this while waiting in a queue or sitting on public transport. A park bench is perfect. Don't attempt it if you are driving.
- Pause all everyday thoughts and silence any distractions. Get into the present moment, even if it seems busy and noisy. The stillness happens within.
- Go within to your deepest center and rest there for a while, for as long as possible.
- Find the place where everything is perfectly still, even if only fleetingly.
- Stay in this place until you have explored it fully. Take the time to access it as much as possible and take strength from the recognition of it.
- After a while, or whenever you need to, emerge from this state and open your eyes again.
- Move forward with your day.

Question: Can we live more positively?
Feeling negative or positive, or however our true selves manifest themselves, can be more or less evident at different times of life, or even from one day to the next, but we must be careful not to let positivity dissipate as time goes by.

Story: A shift of mood
If we want to make changes in our lives, we have to be aware of how we experience things, how we live through things: our reactions may seem too entrenched, too predictable. Where did youthful positivity go? Could it be rediscovered? Where is the real "self" that is "me" or "us"? Is it buried? Perhaps digging

deep might reveal how things could evolve, change, and allow us to live better.

★ ★ ★

The couple walked through a city, observing the subtle changes as they moved from one neighborhood to another. One moment there was poverty; the next, extravagant wealth. More than this, the city held deep within its memory a harshness from the past, a roughness, a violence, and this could be experienced here, now, in the twenty-first century, on the streets, at any moment. This might be part of being located on a fault line. You never knew when it might be your turn to be tossed into the air like a piece of flotsam, detritus, to be battered and scattered against the brilliant blue sky. An old photograph of a man in a ten-gallon hat and spurs came to mind, his white horse carefully picking its way through the smoldering ruins of the devastated city the morning after a disaster. He was like a ghost caught in time, in memory, out of place. That man was long gone, but his essence penetrated the more recent layers and newer foundations, the sturdy walls and sidewalks. Still there. Alive.

The districts morphed from one to another, and all the harshness melted away the moment the couple crossed the street. There was a feeling of being scrubbed, cleansed, relaxed, refreshed. There were shaded spots to sit and sip delicious, fresh coffee, nibble a snack and relax, contemplating the day. The very air seemed virginal. There were no fluttering scraps of litter and every sidewalk seemed lovingly tended. Displays of flowers decorated windows and hallways. Each little table held a beautifully arranged posy. The kerbs were lined with rainbows. The traffic was slow, smooth, quiet, and careful. The couple felt the cares of the world evaporate as their shoulders dropped, relaxed. What was it that they had been so anxious about? They could no longer remember. There was nothing but love here. Nothing.

Activity: Achieving a positive state

Dealing daily with a negative spiral is like diving into the depths, only to realize when you are almost on the ocean floor that there is a surface you can swim up to, that it is real and possible. It's just a question of remembering to come up for air and then actually doing it – choosing to live every time.

- "I feel down." This is a state of perhaps being in a bad mood or depressed. At this point you acknowledge your own feelings.
- "I am down." You realize that you are in a "down" phase.
- "I am on the bottom." You know that you are in a bad place, but you can see that there is a glimpse of hope.
- "I can look up and see the surface and sky." You remember to look away from yourself and your "down-ness" and realize that there are other directions, other ways, and that they are upward.
- "I can swim up to meet it." You realize that you can do something to improve your state and act, now.
- "I will feel better." You can act and you know that you will soon experience improved mood – feeling more hopeful generally.
- "I do feel better." You know you have acted and you acknowledge your improved mood. You realize that you can change your own behavior in life, by yourself, and experience the hope working on your behalf, with the positivity flooding back in.

Question: Can we live more by sensing other energy?

What is there that might be outside the self in life? Another energy, another power? The unexpected. The unknown. Or are we talking about the whole of life, the energy of life within everything that lives? Does it matter? Energy can be just as easily within as without – or both. Much comes down to personal interpretation and mood on the day. Is there time in daily life to consider what this might be and how it might be of importance?

Story: Spooked

Whatever your personal beliefs, being aware of another side of life, or the beliefs of others, can enhance your life in unexpected ways.

★ ★ ★

The tourists found themselves, around Halloween time, looking for a hotel for a couple of nights. They were admiring the beautiful architecture, the soft colors of the paintwork, the intricate ironwork tracery, balconies and shutters, the wafting, trailing foliage, soft breeze, dense heat. The romance of it all was seductive. Several hotels looked promising, so they picked one and wandered in. It was intimate and inviting; charged with atmosphere. The receptionist flashed a wide smile and said that, yes, indeed, they did have a vacancy.

The room was full of charming colonial-style furniture, high four-poster bed, crisp linen, dark wood, chintz, overstuffed armchairs, old prints on the walls, creaking floorboards. It was perfect. A generous, sagging balcony overlooked the street. What a find! The tourists took in their surroundings, becoming gradually conscious of open-topped tour buses, guides speaking into microphones, pausing right under their balcony. They explained all about the hotel, though words were indistinct. Eyes turned up toward the tourists. Feeling exposed, bemused, the couple returned to their books. It felt unsettling to be part of a tourist attraction.

A couple of days later, as the couple were checking out, a different receptionist settled their bill and asked them how they had enjoyed their stay. They asked him about the tour buses. Was the hotel special for some reason? Oh yes, he said, this is the most haunted hotel in town. Hadn't they realized? He smiled broadly. "The others are with us all the time," he said. "They are everywhere." The tourists laughed nervously, quickly picked up their bags, and moved toward the door.

Activity: Experiencing something different with positivity
"Living" presents challenges, which are good to acknowledge and confront. When something different crops up, notice it and look on it as positively as possible. If you feel fearful or out of your comfort zone, try to access your more positive side and move forward with confidence to meet the difference head on.

- Think back to a time when you noticed a different side of life. When you had a sudden realization that life was not quite as you had been experiencing it so far.
- Explore any feelings you had then. Surprise? Recognition? Fear? Amusement? Perhaps there was a confusing mixture of feelings.
- Delve deeply into these feelings and re-experience how you felt then. Try to recapture a sensation of life being full of variety, unexpectedness, and possibility.
- Did it feel like a good experience – or not? Maybe it made you feel unprotected, insecure, or maybe it excited you in the way that going on a new adventure might.
- How does your sense of something different then seem to you now? Was it challenging at the time? Does it feel the same to you now? Or if it was exciting at the time, does it still feel that way to you now?

Question: Can we live in the flow more?
We may become aware of living in the flow only after it has occurred. This is when we re-engage with everyday life and find that time has elapsed without our being aware of it. We were concentrating so deeply on one thing that it has taken

over and carried us into another mental place. This could be as simple as reading a captivating novel. Such moments give deep satisfaction.

Story: A pathway to the flow zone

Personal objects and tools can be valuable routes into the state of personal creative flow. A combination of action and dexterity, sound and touch can collude to create the perfect vehicle for traveling temporarily to another, creative, place in life.

★ ★ ★

The woman had several routes into her personal flow zone, but a particular favorite was her sewing machine, now ancient but still functioning. She felt a personal rapport with it. She could work out how to use such old-fashioned hardware and then put things right, within reason, if they went wrong. She liked the feeling of being able to rip out a snagged bobbin or a puckered piece of material, undo a few screws and sort out the tangle of knotted threads and fluff beneath, hidden in the inner workings. She could feel the fabric move beneath her fingers, making perfectly even stitches, hear the gentle whirr and click of the engine, oiled and primed, ready to make magic in the realm of color and texture. The neatness required to be a good practitioner tested her patience these days, that was true, but she had learnt many personal shortcuts to such refinements. Perfection was for others and she was happy with "good enough." She was only looking for the enjoyable sensation of being carried away with the process, to be buried in it, to become part of it, to be transported by it, out of the real world and into a kind of make believe.

Just seeing her sewing machine sitting there, waiting, had the ability to calm her and lead her gently toward a personal flow zone. Sewing in straight lines, up and down, securing the layers of a cozy new quilt was her preferred way of finding her zone of creativity. She eased the soft, forgiving layers of color and texture, placed pleasingly together, beneath the machine's foot. Before too long, the woman was in her dream space, and her imagination was floating in the space somewhere above her head. The sound of the machine was soothing, putting her in mind of long-held memories of her mother running up summer clothes in the room next door while she dropped off to sleep. It recalled summer evenings, birds still awake, the soft rustle of leaves in the tree, the house settling down after the day.

She was in a daydream, in her creative flow state, and she was removed from reality, into something else, just as real but different. Later she felt refreshed and her mind soothed. Something that could not really be defined had traveled between eye, brain, and fingertips, and back again, in a mysterious way.

Activity: Putting yourself in the path of flow

Being in the flow state will put you in the way of living more fully in your creative self.

- You may not be able to induce a flow state at will, but you can put yourself in its path, so that it happens more easily. You find yourself to be more "alive" and able to live more creatively. It is also an excellent stress-buster.
- Perhaps you are working with your hands, mending something, and listening to a podcast that is transporting you to another place in your mind. Your hands, in their repetitive, soothing activity, are moving from their muscle memory, releasing your mind to do its creative thing.
- The rhythmical activity takes your thinking self to what you are hearing and allows you to concentrate. Creativity and new ideas can spring to life.
- From this point you might start on a wonderful daydream, which becomes ever more embroidered in

your mind – you are in true creative flow, adding layers of light and hope to your life.

Question: Can we live more by trusting more?
Can we face up to our own shortcomings and get over them? For example, do we find it hard to trust others and put ourselves through anxiety because of it? Why can trusting be so hard for us? Is there a truth within that might need looking at? This might be connected with the need to feel safe at all times in life.

Story: The door whisperers
Perhaps we should have more faith in others, so that we can trust more fully and experience more joy in life generally.

★ ★ ★

The new flat was nearly ready, but there were a few things to sort out before moving day. The woman felt strained. Two men came to sort out the doors. She felt she could trust them, though she was annoyed. A headache simmered. She composed a stinging review in her head. There was muttering, even some whispering, which unsettled her. Was something wrong? It could easily be. She was becoming paranoid and felt sick. She started praying about the door, which was now lying on its side, exposing the flat to the outside world. The woman thought about how over-the-top praying was and felt ridiculous and neurotic. Such a first-world problem! No one was dying. She was ashamed of herself, of her fears and lack of confidence in others. One thing led to another, knock-on effects and more sawing, whispering, maneuvering, and adjusting, drilling, tutting, and clicking. Effort. Skill. Confidence. An hour later, the door was rehung, fixed, made new. The woman felt a surge of relief, far greater than the episode merited. She was still ashamed of herself, but felt fully restored to life.

Activity: Remember to breathe

We may find that even though we are aware that we should be doing something regularly and that it works and does us good, we simply forget it exists – or we forget to do it. We might be living, by default, too much on the surface of life and neglecting to plumb the depths. In the moment of panic and reacting to a situation, we probably do the very things that make everything worse – we panic, we hold the breath, we allow automatic reactions to get in the way of acting calmly.

Activity: Breathing to add calm to life

Try these two breathing sequences. It may help to visualize the individual breaths as "arrows," with the point marking the moment where the breath changes from "in" to "out" or "out" to "in." You will find that you feel calmer and more focused.

Variation 1:
- Think "one" as you breathe in.
- Breathe out.
- Think "two" as you breathe in.
- Breath out.
- Think "three" as you breathe in.
- Breath out.
- Repeat the sequence for as long as you like.

★★★

Variation 2:
- Breathe in.
- Think "one" as you breathe out.
- Breathe in.
- Think "two" as you breathe out.
- Breathe in.

- Think "three" as you breathe out.
- Repeat the sequence for as long as you like.

Question: How do we live with a little discomfort?
Perhaps noticing a moment of discomfort can remind you that you can go further down – and further up too. It is as though you are looking for balance. Perhaps there could be downs and ups in life, but not too many of one or the other, and a place in the middle, for most of the time. The small annoyance, or moment of uncertainty, insecurity, is there to allow you to experience something greater. It does not smooth the way forward but it can make you feel more capable, more in control, in charge of your own universe, which you already are. When you know you have gone through a small rite of passage, a sense of relief can feel like the fulfillment of hopeful actions, thoughts and increased confidence. Perhaps a challenging predicament does not look promising at first. There is reticence, fear, lack of confidence, and uncertainty about what to do and how to do it. However, taking courage in both hands can feed us with hope and the feeling that we can do things – and also enjoy them in the process.

Story: Welcome to China!
Experiencing small challenges can bring discomfort, and surely growth in life too.

★ ★ ★

The woman visited China. Her husband was working there and invited her to have a holiday. She had been on a few such trips before and knew that she would need to be prepared to spend time alone, to be adventurous, to fend for herself, and get on with it. He would be busy.

On her first morning, the woman woke long after her husband had gone and she tried to decipher the torn scrap of paper he had left for her (this was before mobile phones). She batted away a rising feeling of abandonment. There was a sketchy map and some hard-to-read instructions. She noticed within a heady mix of fear, courage, and personal empowerment – on top of a feeling of complete freedom.

She made her way, as per instructions, to the subterranean bike garage and set off, feeling weirdly confident. She had nothing to lose. The bike lane was so wide it could take about 20 cyclists across and it was packed. All the woman had to do was steer a straight path, remain upright, and follow the map. A shower prompted a brief pause under a flyover. It was strangely convivial, though no words or glances were exchanged with the other cyclists. She passed through the main square. Huge red flags fluttered and a gigantic statue of Chairman Mao gazed into the distance. "Welcome to China" a young woman said, smiling. A shock of happiness hit the woman and all anxiety drained away.

After a while she arrived at her husband's office, found a place for the bike and made her way, shaking and sweating, to the top of the building, along a few corridors and through a thick metal door. She felt a sense of achievement. A grinning crowd of faces looked up at her as she peered timidly inside. "Well done!" voices cried. "You have passed your first test in China – you are in time for lunch!" Spread out on newspapers was a magnificent banquet of the local cuisine.

Activity: Make an "altar"
Sometimes making a physical focal point can help gather and concentrate your thoughts, giving a center to them to face any challenges. Noticing the "stone in your shoe," the sense of discomfort that has been bothering you, can then be

acknowledged, shaken out, discarded, in order to move on with living. Gathering the items for your "altar" can help calm and focus you.

- Look for things you love, which you would like to pay attention to. Or perhaps you can use things that you don't love, or are about to eject from your life. All are equally valid, but they must have importance for you.
- Find a space for them to sit for a while undisturbed: a shelf, a ledge, a windowsill, or a bookcase.
- Perhaps choose things that have a common theme: a holiday, a feeling, a time or occasion in your life, a person.
- Assemble the items gradually, contemplating each one, thinking about its importance, appreciating its significance or beauty, or both.
- Add items until you are completely satisfied with your composition. Remove those you are not happy with, without further thought.
- Whenever you need to, contemplate your "altar" and feel the way it affects you.
- Experiment by finding different ways of using it. See how you notice it when you come into the room and glance at it quickly, or if you stare at it in meditation, eyes semi-focused.
- Explore your feelings and thoughts.

Chapter 3

Hope

[T]here will ye witness a living Hope.
Margaret Fell

What is hope? A word that is thrown around quite carelessly? It is a word we know means something important, but it is often hard to say exactly what. It seems to contain within it a positivity and perhaps that is all it needs to express. Perhaps it is a living force that moves us upward and onward in the faith that all will be well. It is real, and at times almost tangible, but it is all too easy to lose and forget about too. Perhaps "living hope" is part of faith generally: the assumption that we can act and hold on, knowing that something good will be the outcome in the end. Perhaps it is to live out an awareness of positivity, of noticing, of acknowledging ways forward, when we struggle to find even the smallest trace of hope, when we feel negative about everything, from the trifling to the global. What can help turn things around? Perhaps even the tiniest nudge is important, must be witnessed and taken seriously. For example, passing ten-foot high letters, crudely spray-painted, spelling out "HOPE" on a railway underpass, may be a jolting reminder to just keep going. Hope can be framed in terms of finding acceptance or accepting what life already holds, rather than trying to change what is there or find more. It is also a sense of expectation and trust in change and improvement, assuredness, and confidence in the best way of things; that all will turn out well in the end, which it will. Having or finding hope is about finding meaning in life. We need the tools to do that, but what are they? Is there anything new to discover about how to look at life?

Hope is the life force that always moves forward – it cannot help doing this and it cannot stop. It has its own momentum. It is like a motor idling, not actually moving, perhaps, but just turning over, with the potential to be revved into action. Hope can seem passive, but its presence allows things to whirr along in the background, to have possibility. It has potential. It is alive. Hope is searching for positives – and then recognizing and finding them, and using them.

Hope sets us on a secure path, it contains a certainty, a state of being aware of sureness, even though that certainty cannot always be there. We have to learn how to harness hope while walking in uncertainty, finding out how to work from a place of not knowing and being content in that state, and accepting it.

How can we witness hope today in our lives? Hope is about taking responsibility for ourselves in our own lives, being inspired, being accountable. It's about being empowered to act. Swimming in the living stream of hope is an individual experience, available to all. The significance of an enlightening experience of hope may strike us between the eyes and it comes without warning. We may not realize that this is hope in action, so we need to be attentive to that part of being alive. Perhaps there is a vague awareness of a current of energy moving through life constantly, but embroiled in our mundane ways, we are only aware of it happening occasionally. We dip our toes into it, then withdraw and perhaps forget or dismiss it – until next time. It is important for us to digest and interpret our experience however we see best. That way it stays pure and unique. This kind of experience can offer hope, that there is another view of life. It is living proof of something, but it is up to us to find meaning, for ourselves. This may be hard if our own culture does not give weight to such experiences. Perhaps we could go back to childhood and relive what might have seemed out of the ordinary or just a bit different from the normal everyday. How did we experience and interpret it then, and how do we rationalize it now? Perhaps it carried great meaning as a child, but over the years it has been filed under "something that just happened in childhood," which could never happen again – the result of "imagination." There is the tendency to dismiss what might be misunderstood: to reduce experience to the material, to what can be "proved." However, we must have the confidence to hang on and to believe in its importance: to know that it is real and to give it the credence that it merits. This can give hope and renewal when there doesn't seem to be any.

The questions that follow are about how "seeing," or not "seeing," the "living hope," might help us live more fully. Are we living life to our different full potentials? The questions are supported by short stories from real life, to act as examples and inspiration, and by practical exercises. Choose the ones that speak to you – and go slowly.

Questions about hope

Question: Can we experience hope coming and going?
What can we do to be open to the arrival of hope, to notice it and make use of the moment? Sometimes a feeling of "all is well with the world after all" comes up. It is the awareness of something that feels normal, of being perfectly balanced. This could be hearing the theme tune to a much-loved program or a shipping forecast, sport reports or mastering "tree pose" and finding that balance in the body-mind encourages hope. All carries on as usual and all feels well. Make the most of every surge of hope. Appreciate it fully and remember it, so that you can bring it to mind when you need it.

Story: The waitress
Hope comes and goes of its own free will and so it's important to notice it when it arrives.

★★★

The couple were on foreign ground, out of their depth. They felt insecure. The journey had been long. It had been hard to find this place and there had been no one to ask for directions. A person walking on the street was a rare sight. The place was a mystery – it was called a city, but was really a drifting collection of run-down lodges, motels, and widely spaced homes. All had seen better days. The lodge interior was dark, highly varnished wood, hung with the parts of dead animals, guns, and fishing rods. The fireplace was gloomy, cavernous, surrounded by roughly cut rocks.

The couple located the dining room. No one looked up when they entered, hesitantly, but a friendly woman approached, introducing herself and explaining that she was going to look after them for the evening. Her words were soothing, calming, as she settled them at a table and offered tall padded menus. Heat and dust melted away. She made recommendations and offered drinks. She couldn't do enough for them and they were absurdly grateful. Soon they were eating a delicious dinner. In between, the waitress pushed and bustled around the kitchen, chatting and laughing, experienced and efficient. She seemed supremely capable, in balance with life and full of hope. The couple were brought back into life by her, their hopefulness and positivity restored.

<u>Activity: Hang out washing</u>
If there is outside space and good weather, hanging out washing can bring satisfaction, job-well-done feelings – and hope.

- The washed items are hung out in order of size using nice-feeling pegs.
- The sun shines down, whitening the whites and killing off germs, we hope. Only the sun's energy, as well as one's own, is being used.

- The breeze causes the washing to flap in a satisfying way – the sound comes from long ago, from a country childhood. Sails flapping.

Question: Can we find hope in trusting our "not knowing"?
Being in the "don't know zone" may involve trusting others. This may be where real work happens because this is a place of hope. It may be the only hope. From this place of not knowing comes learning to trust others and whatever "God" is, and knowing that hope has to happen, just as a rubber ball has to bounce back upward when it has been dropped.

Story: Lobster lunch
Sometimes you just have to trust another person to do the right thing, especially when you are in the "don't know zone." There is hope in that action.

★ ★ ★

The family was somewhere on an island, four of them in a hired car. They were conspicuous. They passed through villages. Women selling fresh fish yelled and jumped into the road, trying to flag them down, throwing whole fish through open car windows onto unguarded laps. They decided to stop for lunch. There was a flickering neon sign outside an unprepossessing-looking concrete bunker. The husband walked confidently in and greeted the proprietor in the gloom. They conferred over the menu and the others went outside. The seats were hot to the touch but the table was welcoming and colorful. There was a posy of flowers and fluttering paper napkins. There were no other customers and no one else in sight. The family sat staring at the sea. Palm fronds, soft breezes. Quiet. Peace.

After a few minutes, drinks arrived and a little later a delicious smell of garlic cooking in a small hut a few yards away. Seductive music wafted across. A while later the man emerged, bearing a huge loaded tray. The food was delicious, more delicious than seemed possible. Moods lifted and everything was wonderful. But almost before they had finished, the husband sprang to his feet with "Let's go!" They heard car tires crunch on gravel. The husband's behavior was uncharacteristic, but now seemed a bad moment to challenge him. There was a feeling of threat in the air, as though the sun had gone behind a cloud. He rummaged in his back pocket, extracted notes and thrust them at the proprietor. His rush seemed rude. The family hurried to the car and drove off. When asked about the hasty exit, the husband seemed evasive, possibly wanting to conceal his fears. Later, he pulled out a map and explained about "snow harvests" [drugs trade]. The village was expecting a delivery and the cars had come to greet the boat, which he had spotted approaching on the horizon.

Activity: Try lucky charms

If placing yourself in the "don't know zone" makes you feel insecure, try using lucky charms. These are everyday talismans that can boost you in some indefinable way. Charms, or talismans, offer comfort, light, perhaps a different route toward hope. They are there, at your back, as you try out difficult things or go through nervous uncertainty. They are on your side and by your side. A small smooth pebble picked up on a walk and held in your hand in your pocket can add reassurance and comfort. Or just glancing at an old object from childhood might give you a boost. These things seem important, but only to you. They are charged with your energy and they work to give you confidence and hope. Don't hang on to things that provide the opposite kind of energy – make you feel insecure and don't give you hope. Move them on.

Question: Can finding motivation help us find hope?

Knowing that you want to act meaningfully is a way forward into making a moment of hope work for you. This little sliver of snatched hope is a prayer, a quick concentrated focus. Before you know it and have captured it, it has flown off into the ether – free to do its work. Think of this moment whenever you want to relive it, whenever you need it and want to harness its power. This will help motivate you into action, into positive, hopeful thought patterns, which may last – all day and beyond.

Story: The wardrobe

Small, seemingly mundane, episodes can sometimes take on larger symbolic values. In this case, the object seems to represent aspects of a couple's life together, holding memories of the past but also hope for the future.

★ ★ ★

The wardrobe was huge, more like a little house than a piece of furniture. Its doors made it look like an old shop front, slightly curved, with small-paned windows. It was solid, built to last. In the main hanging area there was just enough space for either winter or summer clothes, not both. The couple had argued over the years about encroaching into one another's space.

They had found this wardrobe in an early flat and now several decades had gone by. It had been used hard: stuffed too full, emptied out in a frenzy of searching for lost items. It kept many secrets, concealed things, and served as a hiding place for small children playing hide-and-seek. It had a personality of its own: kind but firm. It could be roughly treated, but it was wise not to push it too far.

One day the wardrobe had to be dismantled, moved, and then reassembled. The couple were no longer young. Would they even be able to tackle this on their own? The task was put off. They inspected the pieces, patting them lovingly. Some vital pegs were worn away, brackets snapped off.

Summoning patience, the couple maneuvered and manipulated. Both were aware that harsh words could easily find life, but previous experience reassured them that this sort of situation was rarely, in fact, a touch paper. There were false hopes and restarts, pinched fingers and moments of angst. They feared for their backs. Would they have to admit defeat and summon a younger person? Finally, the whole thing clunked into place. It was whole again. The wardrobe seemed to sigh as it rediscovered its old position. Good for a few more years yet.

Activity: Say a little prayer

A prayer is just a small, concentrated moment of complete and utter awareness, of focus, of drawing all your being into one place, with one purpose, with one thought, moving in one direction. It's as easy as that and is almost too simple to notice. It passes so quickly, but just knowing about this possibility can kick-start hope.

Question: Can times of discomfort help us find hope in life?
A time of stress might serve to fuel the energy of hope, after preparing a space in which it can emerge and flourish.

Story: The cake

Hope ebbs and flows. Sometimes its energy is high to begin with, perhaps too high, only to be dashed away, but traces of it always persist.

★ ★ ★

The girls huddled in the departure lounge. They were excited, chatting and laughing loudly. Amongst the muddle of bags, phones, and snacks there lay a large iced cake in a cellophane-covered box. It was on show, to be admired. Just visible, in pink scrolled icing, were the words "Happy Birthday Daddy." The atmosphere was close, the air-conditioning barely noticeable. The group waited for the flight to be called; time dragged. Nothing happened. Anxiety was passed around. Eventually an official with a clipboard unsmilingly beckoned. The group trailed outside; meeting the hot air was like stepping into an oven. Everyone squinted in the white light and trooped across the dissolving tarmac toward a small plane, treading between white lines. The group waited under the shade of the plane's wing. The girls struggled with their bags and the suffering cake. Words flew in the still air.

The plane looked hot, old, and tired. It was hard to believe that it could get everyone up into the air, across the sea, and then safely down again. Someone inside was hitting something hard with a hammer and the whole plane rocked. After a while, a large man emerged dragging an outsized toolkit. It was hard to know how to read his expression. His overalls were soaked and he used an oily rag to mop his shining head. The cake was melting fast, pink icing bleeding. The girls passed it from one to another. What was once a festive surprise was now something that no one wanted to take charge of.

The group climbed into the plane. Moods lifted as confidence returned. The pilot cracked jokes, hands moving confidently, soothingly, as though he was driving a car. The plane lifted, stuttering and shuddering, struggling to gain height. Once airborne it felt powerful, invincible, even. Islands and ocean flowed beneath. Flocks of white birds fanned out. Surf played. The planet, a blue orb, hung in space.

Later, everyone waited outside the airport. There was nowhere to sit and no one about, only an air of dusty abandonment. There were no friendly named welcome cards, but a hire car would arrive soon. All would be well. The heat seemed to invade everything. Eventually, a very old car drew up and we drove away. A glance in the rearview mirror revealed the girls still waiting. The cake box had been laid to one side in the corner, just visible behind the pile of bags, but everyone was laughing.

Activity: Tidy a drawer

There is a drawer where everything is thrown in, without looking. It's a "lazy drawer" and it remains shut, concealing its embarrassing jumbled contents. Its mere presence is uncomfortable. We know what's in it, but no one can find anything when they need it and so no one ever looks for anything in there. They just glance in, shut it quickly and forget about it all over again. It is too difficult.

However, the act of taking everything out, discarding the unwanted, and arranging the wanted, bringing the drawer back to life, is very restorative. It just feels good. The dead area comes alive again and the dead things within take another breath. There is hope. The good feeling, the hopefulness, after you have given such a space back its order is worth all the effort, ten times over.

Question: Might letting go allow hope to return to us?
Perhaps all hope seems lost, in the moment, so the best way forward is to surrender to what is, trusting it will return. Hope may be a way of being willing and prepared to start all over again, time after time.

Story: The conversation

Sometimes hope can return if we let go, releasing the self from whatever it is that is most desired.

★ ★ ★

The woman was driving an oversized car through a city. She knew which way to go, roughly, but was unfamiliar with road layout and local driving laws. Everything was new and different, but not altogether unwelcome or even problematic. It was a challenge she felt she could cope with. The dashboard was a mass of flickering lights and buttons. A map was lying under a pile of toys and bags in the foot-well. She held her nerve. Meanwhile, the little girl gabbled and her mother tried to keep her amused. There was plenty to distract a nervous driver.

Out of the blue, the younger woman started talking about a personal issue. The older woman found it hard to focus on this important information and drive at the same time. She reminded herself to remain calm, be supportive, reassuring, but instead she embarked on a long, rambling spiel. She tried to say something meaningful, useful, supportive. Silence. There were so many ways to interpret what she had just said.

Gripping the steering wheel in hot hands, the older woman returned to the rented house, and the sky had not fallen in. The streets were dusty and charming, trees dripping with trailing creepers. The low evening light was enchanting. She parked the car, unloaded, and went inside.

There was a shift of energy, of release, a return of hope, and the air seemed new, clean, and fresh. A while later, the personal issue was resolved.

Activity: Three small words

If life seems too complex, and your mind whirls restlessly from one issue to another, let go of all the details and focus on three important words that you feel will make a difference in your quest for hope. But you have to make them real every single day, so choose realistic, grounded words, which you feel drawn to, which are already real in your life, but which you need to focus on because they are easily overlooked, forgotten. They could be, for example, "porridge," "yoga," and "kindness," so that you have a range of practical, physical bodywork, and mental work every day. They must be the right words for you. In this case, porridge sustains the body all morning, yoga wakes the body up and calms the mind, connecting mind, body, and spirit. Kindness must be used all the time, all day, every day, without fail. Check at the end of each day that you have responded to, or even just acknowledged the words. If you have not been able to make them a reality today, then they are there, waiting, for you tomorrow and the next day too.

Question: Does acceptance of an ending let hope flourish?
Death or any other kind of ending is another type of letting go. Acknowledging it releases you into the now and lets you come back into the living world, to make the very most of it now, tomorrow, the next day. The past cannot be undone, only learned from. What have we learned? How can we best enjoy the now and benefit as fully as we can? How can we make things better for tomorrow and give ourselves hope?

Story: The wheel of life
Sometimes words do not do the job of transmitting meaning about life, about hope. Instead, you may find that the hope you are looking for is already present and needs no verbal explanation to gain understanding. Perhaps lack of words assists bringing about letting go, so that there can be hope in all of life, especially death.

★ ★ ★

The tourists were standing in front of a mandala, a wheel of life, full of color, vibrancy, and intricacy, on the wall of the monastery, somewhere on a high plateau, on top of the world. The sky was vast, meadows endless, the mountains ranging away to eternity. Nearby hills wore lines of fluttering prayer flags. It was bitterly cold and the air was bright and alive. Colors seemed more intense than normal. In a draughty tent nearby, there were noises off from a crowd of young novices watching old war films and the violent soundtrack made vivid contrast with the monastic peace.

The guide explained everything about the mandala, at length, and the interpreter translated patiently, phrase by phrase, word by word. After a while, it became clear that translating was no longer strictly necessary. Everything could be understood. It was all there. Every single tiny aspect of birth, death, and all of life in between was accounted for and answered to in the wheel, the circle that is the continuous life cycle, going round and round, for ever and ever, in a complete image of connectedness. It seemed to bring acceptance of life, of everything that is, and it pointed toward the hope in all that exists in the never-ending moving circuit, in which all of existence is clearly seen. There was deep acceptance of the circle of life, particularly death.

<u>Activity: Get on your mat</u>
The small act of choosing a space and laying out a mat can fill you with positive intention – this is the right thing to be doing in this moment, regardless of other pressing commitments, the "oughts" and "shoulds." From a place of "yoga" or another floor exercise (the choice is yours) you can contemplate your own mortality and all fears melt away. You are connected with the cosmos and this is how you are meant to be. The sheer act of getting down onto the mat can prompt a shift in mood, a movement within, not just bodily. It can provide hope on a deep level, connecting mind and body.

- Feel the mat's texture beneath your feet and palms. Maybe it's squashy, tactile, sticky. Try stacking two mats for extra comfort.
- Lie on the mat and stare upward and apparently "do nothing," feeling your body almost merging into the floor.

- Try some asanas and stretches, or your preferred floor exercise.
- Upside-down poses can induce calm, which seems to come from nowhere and be nothing.
- Balancing poses can allow you to contact the balance within, keeping you upright and connected to the trueness of life and everything that is.
- Twists can keep your inner workings going well and connect you with your posture.

Question: Might adding ritual bring hope?

Making a conscious effort to add little ritualistic touches and embellishments to life makes all the difference to what might be mundane, taken for granted. This brings an element of magic to your life and, in turn, positivity and hope. Small, intently felt actions, perhaps repeated many times, may help here.

Story: The ritual

Doing things in the same way time after time can add anticipated enjoyment and deeper meaning to an ordinary action or activity. There is much hope to be discovered in looking forward to a well-practiced ritual that you have found to embody perfection itself.

★ ★ ★

The man walked up the beach toward the café. He was in his mid-seventies, deeply sunburned, generously bellied, wearing just a crushed straw hat and a low-slung pair of faded shorts. Aviators shielded his eyes from the harsh sun and a sodden gray plait of hair stuck firmly between his shoulder blades. The heat was intense; no breeze.

He went in to the bar and purchased a single bottle of beer, the kind that can be swallowed easily in just a few gulps, carried it down the beach and into the water with him, holding it tenderly above his head, while the gentle waves lapped gradually up his body. He looked like a modern-day Robinson Crusoe, perhaps, or some other guy who had been washed up on an island for a long, long time. He took a couple of sips from his beer and stared out at the horizon. His thoughts and contemplations one could only but hazard a guess at. His eyes, if they could be glimpsed, would very likely be piercing blue. In his youth he had surely been a slim, blonde heart-stopper, a surfer dude, no doubt.

After about ten or 15 minutes a woman came slowly up the beach, following exactly the same path. She was about the same age, wearing colorful swimwear. She was shapely, heavily bronzed and graceful. She looked as though she was absolutely in command of her life – and perhaps of her partner's too. Very relaxed. She was carefully coiffeured. Stepping gingerly into the waves, she bobbed beside the man. They chatted and laughed. They had been a couple forever, it seemed.

After a long time, they emerged and wandered off again, after returning the empty bottle to the bar.

A few days later, at the same café, at the same hour, the same man took the same path up the beach to the same bar and bought another bottle of beer sporting the same label as before. He was wearing the same hat and shorts too. Holding the bottle above his head, as before, he walked into the water and gazed at the horizon, taking little sips. After about ten minutes the woman, looking the same as last time, arrived and bobbed in the water in the same spot as before. Her position in the shallows relative to her partner was just the same as the previous time.

There was something comforting about witnessing such small actions repeated, presumably many times, perhaps for weeks, months, possibly years. There was a relaxed atmosphere of security, of hope.

Activity: Make soup

Perhaps it is necessary to get active, be productive, to move about. Making things in a well-practiced way is ritualized, bringing added meaning. It is an activity charged with hope.

- Start by looking in cupboards, selecting ingredients, seeing what's there, what needs eating up, what goes with what, what will enhance what, chopping, cutting, measuring out, finding the right cauldron and spoon for stirring, the oils and spices, the delicious herbs.
- As you gradually start heating and adding, mixing and cooking, the aromas start to rise and mingle. You feel yourself becoming ever calmer because you are somehow being removed from your head-held concerns. Your taste buds start tingling. You can feel the saliva. The order of adding things seems to reflect the natural order of life. The act of stirring is like merging your dreams and ideas. New things are released into your head as you gradually incorporate everything in the pot.
- Add stock, stirring all the time with a right-feeling wooden spoon. First one way, then the other.
- Put the lid on and leave to simmer for an hour or so, blending and thickening later. The ideas that are coming to you seem to fall over each other in their haste to be born. How will they come to life? How will they be used?
- Season to taste later and add some embellishments – croutons, chopped herbs sprinkled, grated cheese – it's up to you.

Question: How can we make a habit out of hope?

Turn hope into something that you expect to appear every day; something you can rely on. Make it habitual, just like other habits you may form in your life. That way you can internalize it and make it a reality – a part of you. Finding some kind of silence, and stillness, even fleetingly, can shape the beginnings of a way into finding hope.

Story: Can we find silence?

Perhaps the idea of "silence" is leading us down the wrong path, for it doesn't really exist. Perhaps we could find peace and hope more easily if we looked for "stillness" instead.

★★★

For years the woman had been looking for "silence," which she understood as being an absence of sound. Silence seemed to be something that must surely exist in the physical world – somewhere. But experience showed that this was far from true. Silence could be found in the spaces between sounds, sometimes. However, birds carried on singing, the wind rustled the leaves on the trees, and the traffic carried on a distant background whirr. There was always something making a sound. Perhaps silence was just a fleeting glimpse of a thing that didn't really exist at all, it was just an aspiration.

She pursued the idea of silence, however, and found it here and there in rapidly disappearing slivers of time and space. It was hardly there at all, but still a possibility, she thought. It was there, momentarily, in the hushed expectant moment when the conductor raised the baton in preparation for the first notes of music to sound. It was a demand for both orchestra and audience to focus. And it was there at the end of the performance, when the baton was still in the air, hanging on to that pregnant pause after the music had ended. This seemed to be a scarcely-there, flimsy barricade to hold back the audience, which, like a barely contained wild animal, then leapt forth, uncaged, into enthusiastic applause. The audience could not abide silence, it usually seemed. During the performance they filled any silent gaps at every opportunity with snorts, coughs, shuffles – and applause in surprising places. It was as though silence had to be obliterated because a space, or a seeming nothingness, could not be tolerated. It was too painful. It pointed inward into a dark place of not knowing, of not being, of not existing.

What could be done? Silence would have to be reframed to become something else, a different understanding, because it didn't really exist. It had to be found within, so that absence and peace could be an individual resource rather than an outward form.

One day the woman was standing in the middle of a busy intersection, trying to cross the road. The red man was glowing and traffic rushed by, too fast, too noisily, too dangerously. The place was anything but silent. But for a split second she felt something inside that was a real place of stillness, of peace. The world rushed noisily by, but all was well in her inward space of stillness. It gave her hope.

Activity: Try time-traveling
Try projecting yourself into the future: your own future, using your own vision, your own imagination. Feel full of hope.

- In times of difficulty, when you are trying to find hope, avoid dwelling on negative aspects of the present.
- When you feel a downward spiral forming, or realize you are attaching to negativity, check yourself. Instead, imagine you and your life in the future, doing all the things you love best. This will help you think of the difficulties of today as temporary, of moving along, passing along, drifting away into the past, taking up a place in the rear-view mirror, leading you into a new and realistic, possible, positive life. The way you feel and experience life will become ever more filled with hope.

Question: How can we help build hope in community?
Perhaps you notice there is someone who lights up the room, to whom people gravitate, who seems to have the skill of being able to relate easily to others. If you notice someone being positive, and perceive this as part of their personality, way of being and general nature, take note and learn from their example. Notice how they lift the moods of everyone around them. What is their secret? They have a great teaching of hopefulness for us and for the world.

Story: The swim
Sometimes being in community is problematic. Perhaps there has to be a time of discomfort before the experience of being alive and full of hope comes into focus. Perhaps the contrast between these two states helps us experience the flashes of hope more vividly. Such moments can be easily experienced in group situations. What is the best way to deal with these? You have to be patient, loving, giving – all those difficult things, and notice how perhaps one or two can lead the way and set an example. The result makes the effort worth it. Perhaps there is someone in the group who is unwittingly offering a way to move forward in hope.

★ ★ ★

There was awkwardness in the group. Nothing seemed to gel. Arrangements were confused, decisions hard to make. Little resentments hung in the air. Some of the group members were already good friends and they stuck together in cliques.

Eventually someone with good leadership skills took charge and corralled everyone into a café along a narrow cobbled street. Their positivity and decisiveness set the mood more positively. There was an upwelling of hopeful feelings. The owner was welcoming, expansive, open arms. Big smiles. The group was relieved, grateful, and the members arranged themselves at a long table. People vied for the best spots, where the most fun would be had, the animated conversations, the laughs. There was some jostling, though polite, of course. The younger ones resisted being split up. Who could blame them?

The menu was long and there was discussion about the meal. Sharing or not? Vegetarians or carnivores? Some were heavy drinkers, some teetotal. Some ate like birds; others as though they hadn't touched a morsel in weeks. Dividing the bill would be a challenge. But by then no one would care.

Voices were raised as the day's game was dissected. Heads popped out of upstairs windows but there was little to see and they'd seen it all before anyway. Small cars squeezed past, sometimes gently brushing the backs of chairs. Later, there was scrutiny of the bill and huddled discussions. Two were given the task of dividing it and collecting money.

Next morning, the group gathered on the beach. The sand was perfect, air fresh, sky blue, the sun offered promise. They found an ideal spot, a newspaper, a book, a sunshade, friendly chat before heading for the water. Chilly at first, they got used to it. Taking deep breaths, they plunged in. After the first shock, they experienced a perfect encounter between water and self. Floating, looking at clouds. Calm at last.

Activity: Time for resolution

Think of something to aim for in the future. It may be something that seems unattainable but which you have always wanted, even if this was buried beneath your everyday awareness. A few tentative steps can set you off on a long journey, which will eventually lead to the conclusion that fulfills your aspirations. All you need to do is decide to start. With determination, habit, resolution, the small steps will add up to becoming a big journey, tough but filled with hope.

Afterword

At the end of it all, what can we draw out of all this? Given that we are living in very difficult times and may feel frustrated and powerless to bring about any sort of change, how can we deal with our own lives, feelings and actions in a positive way? How can we exist within and alongside difficulty? Given that the only change we can bring about and have control over, realistically, is within ourselves, how should we *be* in the world? How can we best move on and live in Light? How can we pull the seemingly separate ideas of "witnessing," "living," and "hope" together, so that they are one entity, working as a single, smooth-running inner process?

To have more hope, more faith, in our lives, perhaps first we have to have the awareness of personal "witness" and be able to make use of it ourselves in our lives. This can be followed by the experience of "living" and then the, often unbidden, push toward "hope," a form of continuous rebirth, which can be acknowledged and welcomed more easily. If we put the words of the phrase "witnessing a living hope" together, as Margaret Fell did, we might see that it can become a useful image, a tool to employ over and over again, to help us act and flourish in this world and benefit others too. With Fell's encouragement, we can learn to turn toward and witness the Light, live in it in our faith, and find hope.

Rebirth can happen again and again – as it must. We are given the chance to start all over again, every day. Hope works within us, flaring up at every chance it gets. It is like an ember, barely discernible, which cannot help but try to rekindle itself, to live again and grow. We need to have that same inbuilt reflex by doing the practice of sitting in silent waiting with others, so as not to ignore it, to let the flame die. Perhaps just when we realize we may have been side-tracked and died to the

Light, hope re-kindles and the flame fights its way, upward and outward, flaring into life. It is tireless and relentless; it has resilience and perseverance. For this to happen to us, within, we have to accept the Light into ourselves, so that it can expose the darkness to ourselves – and to others, in honesty and truth. To come alive and remain alive, hope takes a deep breath. And another. It breathes, and breathes in more and more life as time goes by. We can engage with the communal silence of the meeting for worship, the stillness, waiting for the call to act in the Quaker Way.

How can this Quaker Way give us hope, renewing us day by day, week by week? Perhaps it is simpler than we think: the regular practice of sitting in a calm, plain place, in silence, listening and finding inner stillness and waiting without plan or agenda for Light to shine in our darkest places, giving us the hope to be able to act effectively in the world. And after that, we just have to remember it, and do it all again, again and again, week after week, month after month, and year after year. This practice is to ground one's life in faith. And faith brings about hope.

We, each of us, have to find our own way to try to live in hope and in the age in which we find ourselves now it often feels as though we have a lot to deal with in the world. There are so many challenges and there seems to be brokenness in many aspects of life now on this planet. My way of trying to deal with this is not necessarily your way. But, in the words of Margaret Fell, if we can only "turn to the Light" and continue the practice of "witnessing a living hope," making connection between these two ideas, and keep on reminding ourselves of these practices, perhaps we can find belief in love, light, and healing. Then perhaps we can keep on finding it, holding this belief in our quiet moments, in prayers and thoughts. We have to keep on working toward that state and eventually experience and witness a hope that is alive because it is truly lived. Like this, we can carry the practice forward into the future, enabling the vision to find a personal reality, which could turn out to be a way of living in love and life, generosity and community – an active prayer that in the end will allow all of us to make discoveries about what these things really mean, and give us all the ability to live them in truth.

About the Author

Joanna Godfrey Wood has been a Quaker all her life and she attended Quaker school. She recently took the Equipping for Ministry course at the Woodbrooke Quaker Study Centre in Birmingham, UK, which gave her the chance to study the works of Margaret Fell. In her local Quaker meeting her particular ministry is facilitating study groups. She has also written *Travelling in the Light: How Margaret Fell's writings can speak to Quakers today* (The Kindlers, 2019) and *In STEP with Quaker Testimony: Simplicity, Truth, Equality and Peace – inspired by Margaret Fell's writings* (Christian Alternative Books, John Hunt Publishing, 2021) and *In Search of Stillness: Using a simple meditation to find inner peace* (Christian Alternative Books, John Hunt Publishing, 2021). Joanna spent her working life as a book editor.

Bibliography

Askew Fell Fox, Margaret, *A brief collection of remarkable passages and occurrences relating to the birth, education, life, conversion, travels, services, and deep sufferings of that ancient, eminent, and faithful servant of the Lord, Margaret Fell*, J. Sowle, 1710

Note to the reader

Thank you for purchasing *In Search of Hope: A Personal Quaker Journey*. I hope you have found it interesting, inspiring, and useful in your life. If you have a few moments, please feel free to add your review of the book to your favorite online site for feedback.

In friendship,
Joanna Godfrey Wood

THE NEW OPEN SPACES

Throughout the two thousand years of Christian tradition there have been, and still are, groups and individuals that exist in the margins and upon the edge of faith. But in Christianity's contrapuntal history it has often been these outcasts and pioneers that have forged contemporary orthodoxy out of former radicalism as belief evolves to engage with and encompass the ever-changing social and scientific realities. Real faith lies not in the comfortable certainties of the Orthodox, but somewhere in a half-glimpsed hinterland on the dirt track to Emmaus, where the Death of God meets the Resurrection, where the supernatural Christ meets the historical Jesus, and where the revolution liberates both the oppressed and the oppressors.

Welcome to Christian Alternative... a space at the edge where the light shines through.
If you have enjoyed this book, why not tell other readers by posting a review on your preferred book site.

Recent bestsellers from Christian Alternative are:

Bread Not Stones
The Autobiography of An Eventful
Life Una Kroll
The spiritual autobiography of a truly remarkable woman
and a history of the struggle for ordination in the Church of
England.
Paperback: 978-1-78279-804-0 ebook: 978-1-78279-805-7

The Quaker Way
A Rediscovery
Rex Ambler
Although fairly well known, Quakerism is not well understood.
The purpose of this book is to explain how Quakerism works as
a spiritual practice.
Paperback: 978-1-78099-657-8 ebook: 978-1-78099-658-5

Blue Sky God
The Evolution of Science and Christianity
Don MacGregor
Quantum consciousness, morphic fields and blue-sky
thinking about God and Jesus the Christ.
Paperback: 978-1-84694-937-1 ebook: 978-1-84694-938-8

Celtic Wheel of the Year
Tess Ward
An original and inspiring selection of prayers combining
Christian and Celtic Pagan traditions, and interweaving their
calendars into a single pattern of prayer for every morning and
night of the year.
Paperback: 978-1-90504-795-6

Christian Atheist
Belonging without Believing
Brian Mountford
Christian Atheists don't believe in God but miss him: especially
the transcendent beauty of his music, language, ethics, and
community.
Paperback: 978-1-84694-439-0 ebook: 978-1-84694-929-6

Compassion Or Apocalypse?
A Comprehensible Guide to the Thoughts of René Girard
James Warren
How René Girard changes the way we think about God and the
Bible, and its relevance for our apocalypse-threatened world.
Paperback: 978-1-78279-073-0 ebook: 978-1-78279-072-3

Diary Of A Gay Priest
The Tightrope Walker
Rev. Dr. Malcolm Johnson
Full of anecdotes and amusing stories, but the Church is still a
dangerous place for a gay priest.
Paperback: 978-1-78279-002-0 ebook: 978-1-78099-999-9

Readers of ebooks can buy or view any of these bestsellers by
clicking on the live link in the title. Most titles are published
in paperback and as an ebook. Paperbacks are available in
traditional bookshops. Both print and ebook formats are
available online.

Find more titles and sign up to our readers' newsletter at
http://www.johnhuntpublishing.com/christianity
Follow us on Facebook at
https://www.facebook.com/ChristianAlternative